# Buddhist Heritage in India and Sri Lanka

## Rediscovery and Restoration

# Buddhist Heritage in India and Sri Lanka

## Rediscovery and Restoration

R P Fernando

Kaveri Books
New Delhi - 110002

First Published in 2017
ISBN : 978-81-7479-203-7



*Published by*
**Kaveri Books**
4832/24, Ansari Road, Daryaganj,
New Delhi - 110 002 (India)
Ph. : 011-4707 2321
E-mail : info@kaveribooks.com
kaveribooks@gmail.com
Website : www.kaveribooks.com

*Typesetting at* Creative Graphics, Delhi

**PRINTED IN INDIA**

# Preface

Though large numbers of tourists and pilgrims visit the Buddhist sites in India and the ancient cities in Sri Lanka today, few are aware that, before the arrival of the British, the locations of Indian sites were mostly unknown and the Sri Lankan historical cities had been abandoned and overrun by jungle. The story of how, firstly, amateur British Orientalists and then the colonial authorities rediscovered and restored these sites is a remarkable one and is the subject of this book. It will also consider how the British presence affected Buddhism in India and Sri Lanka. At the time of their arrival, the status of the Buddhist faith was very different in the two countries. The religion had been virtually eradicated in India. In Sri Lanka, Buddhism had endured a calamitous period under the Portuguese but the environment had improved somewhat under the Dutch. Though other Westerners were also involved with these activities, this book will focus on the leading role of the British, particularly the outstanding contributions of Sir Alexander Cunningham and Sir John Marshall in India and H C P Bell in Sri Lanka.

The first part considers the legacy of the British for Buddhism in India. It describes the activities of the early Orientalists and the explorations of Alexander Cunningham's early years. It then considers the founding of the Archaeological Survey of India. The bulk of this section consists of the achievements of the Archaeological Survey of India during the directorships of Sir Alexander Cunningham and Sir John Marshall. The second part details the rediscovery and the restoration of the important Buddhist sites at Lumbini, Buddha Gaya, Sarnath, Kushinagara, Sravasti, Nalanda, Sanchi and the Ajanta Caves. This part concludes with an account of the museums in India that were established during this period.

The third part considers the British legacy in Sri Lanka. It describes how after an initial difficult period, Buddhism revived. The major portion of this part is devoted to the restorations of the ancient sites, in particular the work of the Archaeological Survey of Ceylon both in the Bell era and the post-Bell era. The next section is on the British contributions to the study of Pali texts. It concludes with the achievements of the eminent Pali scholars, Rhys Davids, F L Woodward and Lord Chalmers.

Much of the book is based on accounts of the history of archaeology surveys in the two countries in recent publications, in particular, the primary sources in the Bibliography. I have focussed on information relating to the individual sites which I have considered in detail. I have also consulted original publications produced at the time. I have paid particular attention to the views of eminent Buddhists of the period such as Anagarika Dharmapala and W A de Silva.

Hopefully, the book will help the reader to appreciate the extraordinary role of the British in the restoration of the Buddhist heritage in the two countries.

I would like to thank Ray Wright and Anne Carpenter for their help and encouragement.

**R.P. Fernando**

# Glossary

| | | |
|---|---|---|
| Bhikkhu | - | Buddhist monk |
| Chaitya | - | edifice (not necessarily dome-shaped) containing sacred item |
| Dagaba | - | large dome-shaped edifice containing Buddhist relics |
| Devala | - | shrine to gods |
| Dhamma | - | teachings of the Buddha |
| Dharmasala | - | preaching hall |
| Jataka Tales | - | birth stories of the Buddha |
| Mahant | - | Hindu priest |
| Mudaliyar | - | senior official |
| Nayaka Thera | - | senior monk |
| Pansala | - | Buddhist temple complex |
| Parinibbana | - | death of the Buddha |
| Pirineva | - | Buddhist educational establishment |
| Pokuna | - | pond |
| Sangha | - | Buddhist priesthood |
| Stupa | - | small/medium dome-shaped edifice containing sacred items |
| Sutta | - | Buddhist sermon |
| Tipitaka | - | Buddhist scriptures in Pali |
| Upasampada | - | higher ordination of monks |
| Vihara | - | Buddhist temple |

# Contents

# 1
# Legacy in India

Following the death of the Lord Buddha, the first major expansion of Buddhism took place during the reign of Emperor Asoka (272–232 BC). The extent of his empire ranged from Kabul and the Himalayas to a line north of Madras. After his conversion to Buddhism, Asoka became a devout Buddhist and played a vital role for the progress of the religion in his kingdom. Buddhism became the major religion of his empire, though he was deeply tolerant of others. He personally visited all the Buddhist holy sites in India. He built tens of thousands of stupas and viharas throughout India, including at all the holy places associated with the life of the Buddha. He erected large numbers of stone pillars containing his edicts which enunciated the duties of rulers and their subjects. He took a keen interest in the affairs of the Sangha and his support for them was munificent. He convened great assemblies of monks including the Third Buddhist Council. He sent his son Arahant Mahinda to Sri Lanka in 250 BC to introduce Buddhism to the island and the religion spread to most of South East Asia.

Buddhism continued to thrive in India for several centuries following Emperor Asoka's death. During the Gupta period (320–550 AD) Buddhism flourished side by side with Hinduism. Most of the kings of the Pala dynasty were also supporters of Buddhism. It spread to China in the first century AD. When the Chinese explorer Fa-Xian (Fa-Hien) explored northern India in the 4$^{th}$ century AD, Buddhism was flourishing and there were hundreds of Buddhist monasteries. However, by the time the great pilgrim Hiuen-Tsang (Xuan Zang) explored India in the 7$^{th}$ century, Buddhism was in decline and Hinduism was coming back into its own. In parts of India there were intermittent revivals between the 8$^{th}$ and the 10$^{th}$ centuries. Elsewhere, its decline continued due to the rise of a new intolerant Hindu sect, attack by Huns and lack of commitment on the part of devotees. Buddhism fell into oblivion during the centuries of the rise of

Islam in India. The worship of Buddhism was concentrated in monasteries and when these were destroyed by Muslim invaders, Buddhism was not capable of withstanding either the violence of the Muslims or the assimilative influence of Hinduism. By the 13th century, the religion had almost vanished from the land of its birth.

## Early Orientalists

Among the Britons who came to India, from the earliest days there were Orientalists who were fascinated by the culture and history of India. The activities of these early pioneers were limited mostly to the translation and interpretation of ancient texts and epigraphs. They gave glowing accounts of the ancient relics, monuments and architectural remains they saw. Their interest in the remains seldom extended beyond a romantic appreciation of their charm or overawing amazement at the magnificence of the artistic artefacts. It could not be described as a scientific response to the historical evidence. The first systematic and academic study of Asian culture and history followed the founding of the Asiatic Society of Bengal by Sir William Jones in 1784. The aim of the society was: 'to inquire into the history, civil and natural, the antiquities, arts, science and literature of Asia'. The Society held meetings for those with similar interests to share their findings. The Society produced an annual journal, *The Asiatick Researches.* A second journal, *The Journal of the Asiatic Society of Bengal* (JASB) was started in 1832. For the first time there was an institutional focus for the study of Asian antiquities. Jones had arrived in Calcutta in 1783 to be a Judge of the Supreme Court. He immediately started learning and translating Sanskrit. He declared that: 'The Sanskrit language, whatever be its antiquity, is of a wonderful structure; more perfect than Greek; more copious than Latin and more exquisitely refined than either'. His most important discovery was to recognise the relationship between Sanskrit and other Indo-European languages. His research included observations on law, education, astronomy, medicine and botany. He translated from Italian, Greek, Latin, Arabic, Persian, Turkish and Sanskrit. He was truly the father of British orientalism.

Other early Sanskrit scholars included Sir Charles Wilkins, Henry Colebrooke and Horace Wilson. Wilkins and Colebrooke founded the Royal Asiatic Society of Great Britain and Ireland in 1823. The journals of the Royal Asiatic Society and the Asiatic Society of Bengal enabled the regular publication of learned papers on all aspects of Asian culture. Sir Charles Wilkins went to India at the age of twenty as a writer in the East India Company. He rapidly mastered Persian and Bengali and began to study Sanskrit with Indian pundits. He was the first to translate the Bhagavad-gita from the Sanskrit. His *Grammar of Sanskrit* remained the standard work for many years. Colebrooke was one of the greatest patrons of Sanskrit philology. While holding high office as Chief Justice of the High Court of Appeal, he pursued his linguistic researches and at the same time put together, at considerable expense, a fine collection of Sanskrit manuscripts which he presented to the East India Company's library. Colebrooke was typical of many of his British colleagues in India during the astonishing first half of the nineteenth century. His contributions to human knowledge, quite apart from his special study of linguistics, embraced astronomy, law, philosophy, mathematics, comparative religion, agriculture, economics and even mountaineering. Horace Wilson came to India as a surgeon but later exchanged the surgeon's knife for the pen and gown. Of Wilson's many translations and essays on Hindu literature, his most celebrated was his last work, a rendering of the Rig-veda. He was the first occupant of the Boden Chair of Sanskrit in Oxford in 1832.

At the time of the arrival of the British, there were practically no written records in India of the life of the Buddha, the holy places associated with his life or the reign of Emperor Asoka. Buddhism gradually became the object of British academic interest. This was the outcome of the discovery and study of texts in neighbouring countries. Brian Hodgson amassed a large volume of Buddhist manuscripts during his appointment as British Resident in Nepal and donated these to institutions in India and Europe. He wrote on various aspects of Buddhism in the Journal of the Asiatic Society of Bengal. It was apparent to Hodgson that the origin of Buddhism was in India and Buddhism had emerged after Hinduism rather than the other way round. He was the first to delineate the historic division of Buddhism between the followers of Theravada, based on Pali Canon preserved in Sri Lanka and Mahayana which covers other schools of Buddhism practised in the Himalayas and beyond.

Another early Buddhist pioneer was Dr Francis Buchanan. He entered the service of the East India Company as Assistant Surgeon in Bengal in 1794. He was appointed to the post of surgeon at the Company's embassy in Burma. On his return to Calcutta he was posted to various outlying areas of Bengal and he was able to able to complete a paper on the *Religion and Literature of the Burmas* towards the end of 1797, which was published two years later. This was the first serious account of Buddhism in English published since Robert Knox's observations published almost one hundred and seventy years earlier. In it he recounted the life history of the Buddha and the main tenets of the religion. He calculated the dates of the Buddha's life according to the Christian calendar. According to the Burmese, Buddhism had been brought to Burma from Sri Lanka and as Sri Lanka had been Buddhist for many centuries, the religion must have once flourished in India. He also concluded that Buddhism was a separate religion from Hinduism.

Buchanan undertook the great Statistical Survey of Bihar in 1811 during which he came to Gaya. He noticed that though the Hindu temples were of comparatively modern appearance, they seem to have been built of older stones containing Buddhist carvings. He spoke to the Hindu Mahant who was aware of the great antiquity of the site but until recently had not known of its religious significance. The Mahant explained that a few years earlier the King of Burma had sent messengers and they had claimed that this was where Gautama had lived and the pipal tree had given Gautama shade as he sat and meditated. The entire site was in a state of utter ruination. As Buchanan examined the brick chamber he noted Buddhist inscriptions. He saw that in the niches of the pyramidal Mahabodhi temple, there were images of the Buddha. He was told that the Burmese messengers had said that the site had been the centre of religion in India and a great Buddhist king had once resided there and had built the temple. Subsequently the King of the Singhala had planted the pipal tree.

One of the most illustrious of the early British Orientalists was James Prinsep. He came to India as Assay Master of the Calcutta Mint in 1819. He was elected to the Asiatic Society of Bengal in 1830 and served as its Secretary from 1832-38. His initial interest was the study of ancient coins but his outstanding contributions were the decipherment of ancient scripts. By training and inclination Prinsep was a man of science and he brought to all his studies a scientist's mastery of factual details. This enabled him to march from discovery to discovery at a pace which still appears amazing. He was among the first to realise the great significance of the excavations carried out in the Manikiyala Stupa in 1830, which brought to light not only huge amounts of Buddhist relics and sculptures but also coins and inscriptions revealing the existence of the Kushan rulers. During 1834-35, he collaborated (*vide infra*) with Alexander Cunningham in the operations at the Dhamek Stupa at Sarnath. This was the first excavation of an ancient site to have been attempted in India as part of an archaeological investigation.

In the period 1834–37, he unlocked the mysteries of both the Kharoshthi and Brahmi scripts. The latter enabled the decipherment of inscriptions on rocks and pillars found throughout India. These inscriptions were clearly inspired by the teachings of the Buddha and the inscriptions refer to 'King Piyadasi, beloved of the gods'. The question then arose as to who he was. The clue came from George Turnour who had translated *The Mahawamsa* in 1837 in Sri Lanka. This showed that the great Indian Buddhist emperor was Emperor Asoka. The identification of Emperor Asoka was Prinsep's crowning achievement. For the first time in many centuries, India and the world knew of the glorious reign of this Buddhist Emperor of India. Prinsep went on to identify the names of three Hellenistic kings from the Asokan inscriptions found on the Girnar rock. This identification helped to place Indian archaeology for the first time on a secure chronological basis. Sadly he died aged 40 in 1840.

## Cunningham : The Early Years

Alexander Cunningham, who had arrived in Calcutta in 1833 to take up a post as a lieutenant in the Bengal Engineers was one of Prinsep's closest friends. He later became a colossus in the field of Indian archaeology. He and Prinsep collaborated closely in their numismatic studies and he submitted a paper to the Asiatic Society in 1834. His early writings include geographic, ethnographic, numismatic and architectural subjects. He acquired a knowledge of Sanskrit and was particularly interested in following the trails of the early Chinese pilgrims. His work for the East India Company initially involved travelling extensively in the Punjab to determine the source of its rivers. During these travels the identification of ancient places became an abiding interest to him. At the start of his career he also went to Ladakh in Tibet and to Kashmir. The early accounts of his travels display several features of his later writings – a focus on identifying ancient routes, a recognition of the importance of topography, a concern for searching out manuscripts, an attentiveness for documenting architectural and antiquarian remains and an interest in the lives of the people in the places he visited.

Cunningham was interested in following the trail of the Chinese pilgrim, Fa Xian, and he published a letter in the Journal of the Royal Asiatic Society in 1843 proposing to locate the whereabouts of Fa Xian's Seng-kia-shi which Cunningham suggested might be Sankisa village on the north banks of the Kali-nadi. He was interested in following Fa Xian's route seeking out all the Buddhist ruins. During the 1840s, Cunningham also identified a large number of places mentioned by the later Chinese pilgrim, Hiuen-Tsang. In 1848 he published a letter in the Journal Asiatic Society of Bengal proposing to follow the trail of both Chinese pilgrims. According to Cunningham, the deceptiveness of the ancient Sanskrit sources, such as the epics, the *Puranas* and the *Dharmashastras* was shown by their silence about Buddhism. The study and publication of all the existing remains of Buddhism (architecture, sculpture, coins and inscriptions) would add greatly to knowledge of the history of India. He also suggested that the colonial government, itself, should be involved: 'It is a duty which the government owes to the country. The remains of architecture and sculpture are daily deteriorating, and inscriptions are broken or defaced; the sooner, therefore, that steps are taken for their preservation, the more numerous and consequently the more valuable these remains will be'.

In 1851 Cunnigham and Captain F C Maisey explored the Buddhist site at Sanchi. For two months they opened a number of stupas within a seven mile radius of Sanchi. The results of their efforts were published in Cunningham's book, *The Bhilsa Topes.* By the 1850s a number of works had been published on the history and doctrines of Buddhism by textual scholars based on documents from neighbouring countries. In *The Bhilsa Topes* Cunningham drew heavily on earlier research but also emphasised the importance of archaeological evidence for historicizing Buddhism. *The Bhilsa Topes* was the first detailed examination of the history of Indian Buddhism which included archaeological evidence from Buddhist sites in a substantial manner.

At the time there was considerable confusion among scholars on a number of issues – the place of birth of the Buddha, the historicity and the dates of the Buddha, whether or not Buddhism had a history before Gautama, on the relationship between Buddhism and other Indian philosophical doctrines and religions. Cunningham's central focus was the history of Buddhism in India – its rise, spread and decline. In the book he addressed a number of important subjects – the life of the Buddha; a synopsis of the Buddha's doctrine; the social impact of his teaching; the factors that attracted women to the religion; Buddhist Councils; monastic rules; Buddhism in Asoka's time and its decline.

*The Bhilsa Topes* shows that Cunningham's lifelong fascination with Buddhism was based at least in part on a strong admiration for the Buddha. This admiration for the Buddha and his teaching is clearly revealed with the contrast Cunningham makes with the purity of Buddhism and 'the corrupt state of Brahmanism'. He also made the following comparison between Muhammad and the Buddha: 'The former propagated his religion by the merciless edge of the sword; the latter by the persuasive voice of the missionary. The sanguinary career of the Islamite was lighted by the lurid flames of burning cities; the peaceful progress of the Buddhist was illuminated by the cheerful face of the sick in monastic hospitals, and by the happy smiles of travellers reposing in Dharmasalas by the roadside. The one was the personification of bodily activity and material enjoyment; the other was the genius of corporeal abstinence and intellectual contemplation'.

There were several sensational discoveries made at Sanchi. Stupa 2 contained the relics of Arahants Sariputta and Mahamoggalana. Other relics of these monks were found in Stupa 2 at Satdhara. Here was important evidence of the historicity of two monks who played an important role in Buddhist tradition. The relic boxes, caskets and the relics themselves found at Sanchi and other neighbouring sites are carefully described and illustrated in *The Bhilsa Topes*. Cunningham identified Sanchi with Sha-chi of Fa Xian's account. He gives detailed descriptions of the stupas, the sculptures and the pillars. In one of the pillars he recognised an Asokan inscription and gave its text and translation. *The Bhilsa Topes* remains an important and indispensible reference work of the archaeology of early Buddhist monastic centres.

The book closes with a poem by Cunningham that reveals his excitement, joy and pride at the discoveries at Sanchi:

> Nought but the Topes themselves remain to mock
> Time's ceaseless efforts; though they proudly stand
> Silently and lasting up their parent rock,
> And still the cities under the magic's wand;
> Till curious Saxons from a distant land,

Unlocked the treasures of two thousand years,
And the lone scene is peopled; - here a band
Of music wakes the echoes; and there the cheers
of multitudes, alive with human hopes and fears.

Fig 1 - Sir Alexander Cunningham (1814 - 1893)

By now Cunningham realised that what was needed at that time for Indian archaeology was a closer and more systematic investigation to bring out a wealth of details. Cunningham submitted a memorandum to the Viceroy, Lord Canning. He stated that it would redound to the 'honour of the British government to institute a careful and systematic investigation of all existing monuments of ancient India'. The proposed investigation was based on Hiuen-Tsang's itinerary which covered not only Buddhist monuments and places but also the Brahminical remains in so far as they were related to the Buddhist sites. Canning readily agreed in December 1861 to fund Cunningham and an assistant for two seasons, 1861 and 1862, to survey north India. Cunningham was formally appointed Archaeological Surveyor for the Government of India in January 1862 and he retired from the Army with the rank of Major-General to take up the appointment (Figure 1). The first government-sponsored Archaeological Survey of India was established.

## Archaeological Survey of India : The Cunningham Era

Cunningham eventually produced twenty three volumes of archaeological survey reports. The first two cover his surveys between 1861 and 1865. Cunningham began his operations in the manner he proposed to Canning. He travelled with the accounts of Fa-Xian and Hieun-Tsang in his hand and scoured the landscape for all the places they mentioned (Figure 2). However, he did not limit himself to the itinerary of the Chinese pilgrims. Twenty five sites are mentioned in the first report and he began his investigations in Bihar. His first report contains some of the earliest and

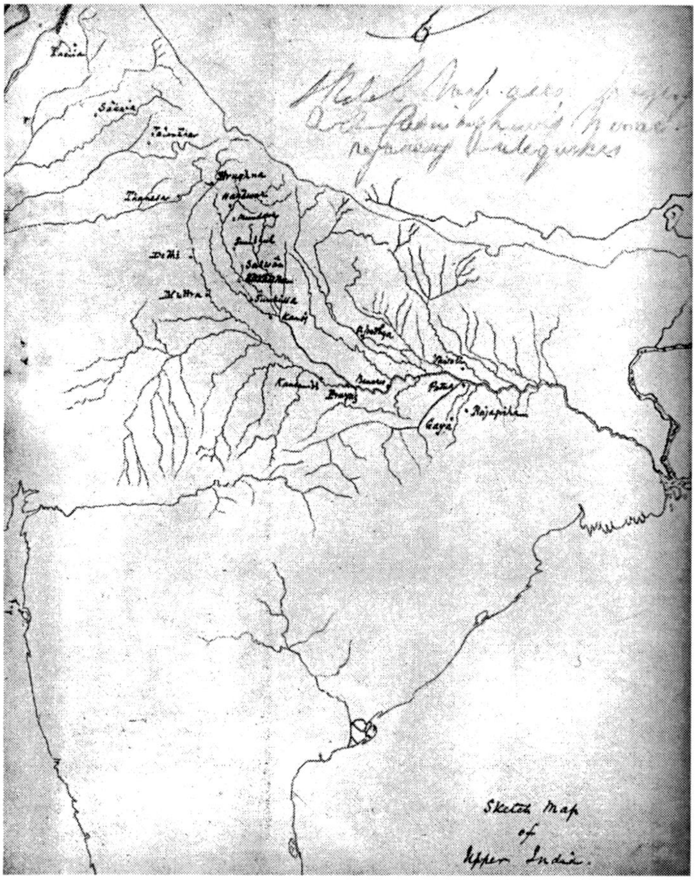


Fig 2 - Archaeological map of northern India by Alexander Cunningham

most careful descriptions of important sites in eastern India including a concise account of Bodh Gaya. He provides a description of Bargaon which is the location of Nalanda. He identifies ancient Pava which was the last resting place of the Buddha before he reached Kushinagara. The survey also located Kushinagara where the Buddha attained parinibbana. Here he found the ruins of an ancient city with a large number of stupa mounds in the vicinity. The reports also contain detailed descriptions of Asokan pillars. Another important site he visited was Sarnath. Cunningham's descriptions of Sarnath are particularly important as he gives an account of earlier excavations, including his own one in 1835-6.

In the season 1862-63, he toured the north-western provinces including Delhi. The major Buddhist site he discovered was Sahet-Mahet which he identified as Sravasti. His excavations of the Jogini- baria mound enabled him to identify it as the site of the Jetavana monastery. At Ramnagar, which he identified with Ahichchhatra, he found one of the largest historical mounds in India. He excavated the mounds and discovered ruins of at least twenty temples. The ruins of the great stupa corresponded to the description of the stupa in Hiuen-Tsang's account. His explorations in 1863-64 were concentrated in the Punjab. He discovered the ancient city of Taxila near Shah-dheri. There were remains of many stupas and monasteries on all sides. He identified one of the stupas at the Buddhist site at Manikyala where the Buddha is supposed to have offered his body to assuage the hunger of tiger cubs. He found further Buddhist remains including stupas at Balar, Tarnawa, Kurmal, Rawalpindi and Gajipur. The region surveyed in the 1864-65 season covered parts of Rajputana and Malwa. He explored the Buddhist caves at Kholvi. He also put forward a general observation on stupa architecture – a chronology of stupas based on the relationship between the height and the diameter of the structure. As an engineer this aspect would have been of particular interest to him. The was general tendency of increasing height with time but there were other stylistic features depending on region which also had to be taken into account.

Though Lord Canning's initial two year time-limit for the surveys was extended, after the 1864-65 season it was not extended further. In this first period Cunningham had systematically surveyed and documented over 166 sites in northern India. By excavating he had identified many ancient cities and religious sites. A wealth of epigraphic and numismatic evidence had helped to reconstruct the early history of India. Cunningham left for England in 1866. The need for further systematic surveys was made to the government from many quarters and in 1870 the Duke of Argyll, the Secretary of State, wrote of the necessity of centralising archaeological activities under the auspices of the government and placing them on a secure financial basis. The Government of India under the Viceroy Lord Mayo accepted the suggestion and a new central department, the Archaeological Survey of India, was established and Cunningham was appointed its first Director-General. The Viceroy's minute stated: 'The duty of investigating, describing and protecting the ancient monuments of a country is recognized and acted on by every civilised nation in the world. India has done less in this direction than almost any other nation, and considering the vast materials for the illustration of history which lie unexplored in every part of Hindoostan, I am strongly of the opinion that immediate steps should be taken for the creation under the Government of India of a machinery for discharging a duty, at once so obvious and so interesting....... I think the time is come when a great and enlightened Government can no longer neglect contributing to the archaeological literature of the world, the result of systematic investigations into monuments and remains, which, perhaps are unequalled in their historic and architectural value'. Cunningham was given a staff of two officers, J D Beglar and A C L Carlleyle.

The government recommended a change of approach. Plans and photographs should be taken and chosen with greater care and negatives in all cases be obtained. Cataloguing and describing of works of art should be pursued more methodically. Antiquities should, as far as possible, not be removed from their original site. The government acknowledged the responsibility of preventing the destruction of antiquities by its own officers. The government also expressed a desire that intelligent 'natives' should be employed in, and trained to, the task of photography, measuring and surveying buildings, directing excavations and deciphering inscriptions. Cunningham returned to India in 1871 and took up his post of Director General. The Archaeological Department's activities were largely confined to northern and central India. A separate Archaeological Survey of Western India was set up under the direction of James Burgess in 1873 and in 1881 this was extended to cover southern India.

Cunningham's Memorandum of Instructions to his two assistants is an important document in the history of Indian archaeology. In it he gave a detailed, systematic exposition of his understanding of the scope of archaeological inquiry. Archaeology, he stated, was not concerned only with broken sculptures, old buildings and mounds of ruins. The study of architecture was as important but not the only part of an enterprise which extended to 'all ancient remains whatever that will help to illustrate the manners and customs of former times'. Cunningham and his two assistants travelled on foot, horseback, elephant, camel, palanquin and, later, increasingly by rail to scour town and countryside for ancient sites and remains. In the 1871-72 survey, Belgar was sent to Delhi and Carlleyle to Agra. One of the places Cunningham surveyed was Buddha Gaya. He had briefly described the site in his 1861-62 report but in the latest report he gave a more detailed discussion of the site including his own excavations and those undertaken at his recommendation by Major Mead. He also went to Rajgir to reconsider the identification of the Sattapani cave as the place where the first Buddhist Council took place. He re-iterated his identification of the Son-bhandar cave with the Sattapani cave. He excavated two further Buddhist sites at Kiyul and Nongarh.

While Cunningham always recognised the importance of epigraphic evidence, the emphasis on it increases in his writings after 1871. In the 1871-72 report he lists inscriptions at Mathura, Buddha Gaya and other places. These are accompanied by translations or summaries and a discussion of their bearing on dynastic history.

His 1872-73 survey concentrated on the Punjab and Yusufzai. In his report he reaffirmed the accuracy of his earlier identification of Shah-dheri with ancient Taxila. During this visit to the site, he excavated several Buddhist viharas and he also found bases and capitals of some Ionic columns of pure Greek design. He made a thorough examination of the Manikyala stupa. He provided a detailed description of the stupa and a sketch of a section clearly showing coins found at different levels. Near the stupa he found two huge Buddha heads made of sandstone. He also discovered important material about several Asokan pillars. This included text and translation of records at two pillars in Delhi. It was during this survey that he made his most important discovery, the ruins at Harappa, but their significance eluded him completely. He thought it was a Buddhist site but half a century later it was identified as one of the most important ancient cities of the Indus civilisation.

His surveys in 1873-74 and 1874-75 were of the Central Provinces. The most spectacular discovery in the first survey was the magnificent Bharut Stupa on which most of the principal events of the Buddha's life were sculptured and inscribed. The stupa is located about two hundred miles northwest of Sanchi. As a result of the excavations here, Cunningham was approached by a Buddhist priest from Sri Lanka named Subhuti who was able to explain many of the scenes shown in the carvings at Bharut and Sanchi which illustrate the Jataka tales. Cunningham also contacted the Ceylon Asiatic Society for further explanation of the Jatakas depicted on the sculptures at Bharut. R C Childers and Mudaliyar L de Zoysa were able to provide valuable information. It was clear that both Sanchi and Bharut were part of a network pilgrim trails that traversed northern India and connected the many thousands of stupas built during the reign of Emperor Asoka. He also discovered Buddhist caves at Bhandak and Wijason.

In 1875-76 and 1876-87 he surveyed the Gangetic provinces. One site he revisited was Sahet-Mahet, ancient Sravasti, to excavate the Jetavana monastery. He spent eleven days at the site. Excavations were made in twenty mounds. Ten revealed remains of temples, five of stupas and five of dwelling houses. He also explored Tandwa with its major ruins including a stupa west of Sravasti. The 1878-79 survey toured the Punjab. The sites visited included Taxila and further excavations at Manikyala. His description of Manikyala included a map, a plan of one of the stupa-vihara complexes and sketches of various antiquities including a relic casket. He identified other Buddhist structures in the area around Manikyala. His tour of 1879-80 brought him back to Bihar and Bengal. He revisited Bodh Gaya but did not undertake further excavations. He did discover a brick stupa at Sultanganj on the Ganges. Excavations here led to the discovery of the famous copper image of the Sultanganj Buddha. The 1880-81 surveys were confined to Bihar. He revisited Bodh Gaya. His excavations at Besrah (ancient Vaishali) yielded several Buddhist artefacts. Nearby at Bakhra he studied the Asoka pillar and discovered a brick stupa. The tour of the Central Provinces in 1881-82 did not discover any significant Buddhist sites. During the survey of eastern Rajputana in 1882-83, he assessed the temple site at Dubkund and suggested that it was Jain and not Buddhist. In his report he considered the Brahmanical persecution of Buddhists and Jains and concluded that 'persecution was as rampant among Hindu priesthood as among the most bigoted of Musalmans'. His final tours in 1883-85 were in Central India and did not include any significant Buddhist sites.

In addition to his annual Survey Reports, he published a number of other books which deserve special mention. While Director General he published the following works – *The Ancient Geography of India* (1871), *Inscriptions of Asoka* (1877), *The Stupa of Bharut* (1879) and the *Book of Indian Eras* (1883). *The Ancient Geography of India* contains all his findings of several decades of investigations into India's historical geography. The subject of his book was mainly the Buddhist period in India. He considered his major achievements were the identifications of Aornos, Taxila, Sangala, Ahichchhatra, Srughna, Bairat, Sankisa, Sravasti, Kaushambi, Padmavati, Vaishali and Nalanda. The Stupa at Bharhut gives detailed descriptions of the structural remains, sculptures and inscriptions at the Buddhist site. A particular feature of the book is the number of well-produced photographs of the sculptures contained in it. The book embodied the first attempt to interpret the relief sculptures at Bharhut. His understanding of Buddhism was based on publications produced by other Western authors. For the translations of the Jataka tales, he relied heavily on his friend, the Sri Lankan Buddhist monk, Subhuti. After he left India he published several books including *Mahabodhi* (1892) which is a comprehensive account of the monuments, sculptures and inscriptions found at the Mahabodhi temple in Bodh Gaya. His overall list of publications is very impressive both in terms of number as well as diversity. His scholarly output is all the more remarkable given the time constraints he was working under. In the first part of his career he was still a serving army officer and after he was appointed Director General he had to spend a considerable amount of time undertaking surveys.

Cunningham's reports frequently make mention of Indian scholars especially Rajendralala Mitra. He also relied on scholars such as Bhagwanlal Indraji and P C Ghosh for translations of inscriptions. He consulted his friend Babu Deva Sastri on matters of ancient chronology and for understanding Buddhist texts and narratives he consulted Subhuti, the Buddhist priest from Sri Lanka. Such positive mention of contribution made by 'natives' was unusual for European scholars in the nineteenth century. Cunningham was an unusual and exemplary archaeologist, in addition to pioneering historical inquiry in the subcontinent. Cunningham retired in 1885 and returned to England and was knighted in 1887.

It is difficult to overestimate the value of Cunningham's great pioneering work in the field of Indian archaeology. He was one of the first to stress the importance of fieldwork, accurate description and precise measurements. He shared with Prinsep the honour of liberating archaeology of its literary and antiquarian afflictions. His ideal of survey-work was comprehensive enough to include every site that was of promise and every antiquity that was of interest. He was responsible for evolving a uniform system of recording under which the description of each building was accompanied by an account of its history and purpose, of its mode of construction, of the nature and colour, of its material and even the mason's marks on the stone. Above all, he was prompt in publishing his results, as is amply testified by the twenty-three volumes of his survey reports, which in Lord

Curzon's elegant prose: 'constitute a noble mine of information in which the student had but to delve in order to discover an abundant spoil'. The *Centenary Volume of the Indian Museum* noted: 'There was no department of Indian antiquities which his master hand had not touched, and everything he touched, he touched but to adorn'.

Fig 3 - Sir John Marshall (1876–1958)

After Cunningham's retirement James Burgess was appointed to the post of Director General. He and J D M Beglar, A C L Carlleyle and H H Cole carried on the work of the Department but on a smaller scale. The work was reinvigorated by the appointment of Lord Curzon as Viceroy in 1899. Curzon's viceroyalty was a dawn of a new era for Indian archaeology. He was deeply interested in the study of Indian antiquities. He was particularly committed to the restoration of the Taj Mahal. He announced the archaeological policy of his government within a few weeks of his arrival. He identified the three cornerstones of the work of the department as being epigraphy, conservation and research. He clearly foresaw an increased government responsibility: 'I hope to assert more definitely during my time the Imperial responsibility of Government in respect of Indian antiquities .... to be faithful guardian of the priceless treasure house of art and learning that has, for a few years at any rate, been committed to my charge'. John Marshall who had previously worked in Greece, South Turkey and Crete was appointed Director- General in 1902. Alexander Cunningham is rightly referred to as the Father of Indian Archaeology in the 19$^{th}$ century and John Marshall deserves this accolade in the 20$^{th}$ century (Figure 3).

## Archaeological Survey of India – The Marshall Era

Several major administrative changes were made from the start. The Ancient Monuments Preservation Act was passed in 1904 that ensured the preservation of ancient sites and prohibited the traffic of antiquities to and from British India. There were also provisions for keeping moveable antiquities in situ or preserving them in local museums. An innovation with far-reaching effects was to institute two scholarships, one in Sanskrit and one in Arabic for giving Indian scholars training in Archaeology. The aim was to enable Indians to be appointed to senior positions in The Survey. Marshall also felt that The Survey should not be renewable annually and should be a permanent government department and in 1906 Secretary of State agreed. He also formulated a new conservation policy that: 'Although there are many ancient buildings whose state of disrepair suggests at first sight a renewal, it should never be forgotten that their historical value is gone when their authenticity is destroyed, and our first duty is not to renew them but to preserve them'.

Marshall was determined to recruit 'men of best scholarly tendencies' to the service. The first Sanskrit scholar, Pandit Daya Ram Sahni, became the first Indian Director-General in 1961. He was the second person to succeed Marshall, the first being H Hargreaves. The first Arabic-Persian scholar was Ghulam Yazdani who spent most of his career as the Director of the Nizam of Hyderabad's Department of Archaeology and undertook splendid professional work at Ajanta. Other early recruits were Henry Cousens and Alexander Rea in Western and Southern India, J.Ph.Vogel in Punjab, Dr T Bolch in Bengal and Taw Sein Ko in Burma. But the real acquisition was Sir Aurel Stein who combined duties of Archaeological Superintendent of the North-West Frontier with those of Inspector-General of Education. Other Indian recruits, who served the Department with distinction, were Dr D R Bhandarkar, K N Dikshit and M S Vats.

Throughout his tenure as Director-General, Marshall succeeded in increasing the capabilities of the Department. In 1921, the strength of the Survey was reinforced by the creation of two additional Superintendent and Assistant Superintendent posts. The decision was taken that henceforth sixty percent of posts must be filled by Indians. In 1926, he was able to arrange permanent funding for the Survey without having to rely on an uncertain annual budget voted by the Legislature. In the same year he obtained approval for four additional officers, a Deputy Director-General and three Assistant Superintendents to help in the work of exploration. This transformation in the scope of the Department was the result of Marshall's unparalleled devotion and commitment and the imagination and industry which he had brought to bear on the task of building up Indian archaeology. Eloquent proof of his early insight was shown in his note produced on the day he took office on 'The Operations and Future Conduct of the Archaeological Survey' (Apr 1903) which formed the basis of all his future programmes relating to preservation, exploration, epigraphy and maintenance of museums.

His major administrative reforms are dwarfed by his achievements in the fields of survey and exploration. Indeed the projects which were undertaken or accomplished by Marshall and his colleagues were so colossal both in their scale and in their number and so extraordinary in their complexity, richness and far-reaching effects of their yields that it is possible here to only give a general trend which characterised them. He first surveyed well-known Buddhist sites like Sarnath and Kasia, Sravasti, Rajgir, Vaisali, Sanchi, Takht-i-Bahi and Shahji-ki-Dheri. The reason for this was that the Survey at the time was better informed – thanks to the Chinese pilgrims and Cunningham's surveys – about these sites than about others. Marshall felt 'it was safer to start with these and make some of our ground before groping our way further into the unknown'. He also believed he was 'more likely to get spectacular finds on these Buddhist sites than anywhere else and such finds were indispensible to us, if we were to interest the public in our work and secure adequate funds for it'.

Subsequent events more than vindicated his hopes. Most of these sites yielded a rich harvest of monuments, sculptures, reliquaries and other antiquities which captured the popular imagination thus making it much easier to extend enquiries to other fields of archaeology which otherwise might not have been possible. Sarnath yielded a rich crop of stone sculptures including the famous lion capital, a colossal Bodhisattva image from the reign of Kanishka and huge hoard of Buddhist images dating from the Gupta age. Sravasti likewise yielded a number of brick-built stupas and shrines, in the debris of one of which was found a group of more than three hundred terracottas depicting scenes from the Ramayana. The excavations at Sanchi revealed more than fifty-one edifices till then hidden under debris. At Nalanda, the Survey explored a vast complex of religious buildings, occupying an area more than 2000 ft by 700 ft consisting of harmoniously planned rows of stupas, chaityas and monasteries. At Shahji-ki-Dheri were discovered the remains of the Kanishka stupa which yielded many treasures including a relic casket of guilt bronze beautifully decorated with seated Buddhas, garland carriers and geese, displaying a harmonious blending of Indian and Hellenistic art motifs. Equally rewarding were the excavations carried out in the Buddhist settlements near Taxila, particularly at the Dharmarajika stupa, where a large number of minor buildings were uncovered surrounding an ancient stupa erected by Emperor Asoka and at Julian which contained beautiful stupas and monasteries embellished by stucco figures of the Buddha. These excavations gave a lucid picture of a new type of Buddhist establishment which developed in the northwest and consisted initially of an open air stupa of imposing dimensions with a variety of buildings surrounding it.

Marshall spent more than twenty years excavating Taxila, which had already been explored by Cunningham, and he was able to obtain the most comprehensive and instructive results portraying urban life in northwest India from seventh century BC to fifth century AD. He was able to expose three successive cities. He came personally to Sri Lanka in 1917 to present a relic casket excavated from a stupa at Taxila to the Buddhists of Sri Lanka as gift from the Government of India. The relic casket enshrined in a golden casket was handed over, with much ceremony, at the Temple of the Tooth in Kandy. His most outstanding discovery remains the ancient city of Harappa in the Indus valley.

Marshall was responsible for establishing a large number of museums under direct control of the Survey including those at Agra, New Delhi, Delhi Fort, Mandalay and at the excavation sites at Taxila, Harappa, Sarnath and Nalanda. Once started, the museum movement expanded rapidly and new museums were founded at many places including Bijapur, Sanchi and Dacca. During the British period over a hundred museums were opened in India, Sri Lanka and Burma. Marshall also established the Central Archaeological Library. Marshall helped to design the Sri Dharma Rajika Vihara thereby earning Anagarika Dharmapala's heartfelt gratitude which he expressed as follows: 'Thanks of the Maha Bodhi Society are due to Sir John Marshall, Director-General of Archaeology, for the kind-hearted sympathy and inspiring advice given to the General Secretary throughout the construction of the Vihara'. He continued: 'The construction of the Sri Dharma Rajika Vihara and the enshrinement of the Holy Relic presented by His Excellency the Viceroy of India to the Maha Bodhi Society is full of significance. On the 26th November 1920, the Compassionate Lord re-enters India after an absence of seven centuries. The Maha Bodhi Society, planted the seed nearly 30 years ago, the seed sprouted watered by the generous hearted admirers of the Tathagata, and it bore fruit on the memorable day when His Excellency Lord Ronaldshay, Governor of Bengal, handed the Holy Relic to Sir Ashutosh Mookerjee, President of the Maha Bodhi Society, to be enshrined in the Sri Dharma Rajika Vihara'. The Anagarika considered this vihara to be the first Buddhist edifice built in India for seven or eight hundred years.

The Anagarika, who championed the Buddhist cause in India, greatly valued Marshall's leadership of the Archaeological Department as noted in the following tribute paid at the founding of the Archaeological Department in Hyderabad in 1914: 'The Imperial Archaeological Department under the directorate of Sir John Marshall is doing a religious work in conserving the ancient buildings in different parts of British India. Sir John Marshall is indefatigable in his labour of love. A classical scholar, and an archaeologist with a scientific knowledge of architecture he has been able to do so much in restoring the neglected buildings of antiquity in India. Under his supervision the Sanchi Topes are being gradually restored, and excavations are being carried on at the site of ancient Taxila in the Rawalpindi district. Sir John has also been able to influence the high officials in the State of Hyderabad, and thanks to Sir Alexander Pinhey, the British Resident in Hyderabad, it has been possible to form an Archaeological Society under the patronage of His Highness the Nizam'.

Marshall relinquished the post of Director General in 1928. He stayed on to write a series of monographs and co-ordinate the results at the excavations at Taxila till he retired in 1931. He was re-employed on special duties and left India in 1934.The foundations of Indian, historical archaeology were laid during his period. The large exposed and conserved sites we see, the gardens around the monuments we appreciate, the museums we enter and the objects we admire, the historical accounts we read are very much the products of 'the John Marshall period' in the history of Indian archaeology.

# 2
# Restoration of Individual Sites

## Lumbini

For many years, the site of the birthplace of the Buddha proved elusive. This was one Buddhist site Cunningham failed to locate. He tracked the Chinese pilgrims too far south. Several people came close to finding it. Vincent Smith, the prominent archaeologist, in 1885 was a magistrate in Basti, about one hundred and twenty five miles north of Benares. In that year, Mr D Ricketts, a manager of an estate with land extending across the Nepalese border, informed him that there was a stone pillar sticking up out of the ground north of his bungalow in Nepal. British officials were not able to go to Nepal so Smith asked for a rubbing to be made of the inscription. Unfortunately, this was identified as 'medieval scribblings' and Smith did not investigate further. Working independently, Dr L A Waddell, a medical officer in the Army based in Darjeeling, was also interested in Tibetan Buddhism and had an abiding interest in tracing the footsteps of the Chinese pilgrims. He, too, was convinced that Cunningham had misidentified the trail of the Chinese pilgrims in this area and was interested in identifying the Buddha's birthplace. However, there was a limit on how much time he could be released from his duties for exploration. He helped discover the remains of an emperor's palace near Patna in 1892.

Meanwhile in 1893 Major Jakaran Singh, an officer serving the Government of Nepal, while hunting close to the Indian border at Nigliva was taken by villagers to a broken pillar of polished stone sticking out of the ground. At the base of the pillar, he noticed four lines of ancient writing. The Nepalese government asked the Government of India for help in deciphering the text. The colonial authorities for the North-Western Provinces and Oude sent their Archaeological Surveyor, Dr Alois Fuhrer to investigate. He located the pillar, recognised the text as Asokan Brahmi and took two rubbings. The inscription on this pillar indicated that this was a pillar dedicated to an earlier Buddha. Dr Waddell compared this finding with Hiuen Tsien's writings and realised that this pillar was close to Kapilavastu which was the location of the Buddha's ancestral home which in turn was close to Lumbini. Waddell wrote to the Secretary of the Asiatic Society of Bengal informing him of the importance of the pillar but was told that nothing could be done till their next planned meeting. Exasperated by the reply, Waddell wrote an article to the Calcutta *Englishman* entitled: 'Where is the birthplace of the Buddha?'. In this he declared that they now stood 'on the verge of one of the most important Indian archaeological finds of the century'. There were difficulties for Waddell to get leave to undertake an expedition himself so wrote to the British Resident in Kathmandu who asked the local regional Governor, General Khadga Rana, to investigate the earlier pillar spotted by Duncan Ricketts in 1885. The two of them watched the Nepalese sappers dig down around the sides of the column till they reached the base at a depth of twelve feet.

Dr Fuhrer who had been asked to join them rushed over and realised it was an Asokan pillar which bore a five line Mauryan inscription: 'Devanam Piya Piyadasi (Asoka) came himself in his twenty-first year and paid reverence here. And, he put up a stone pillar, with a horse on it, on the ground that the Buddha, the Sakya sage, was born here...'. The pillar was at the base of a small hill on which there was a shrine erected in honour of a local deity. In 1897, two of Vincent Smith's ICS subordinates obtained access to the shrine and in it they found the recumbent figure of Maha Maya, the Buddha's mother, represented in bas-relief, as just having given birth to the Buddha. This is the site of the Maya Devi temple. An old bathing pond was also found close to the pillar. After examining the Lumbini pillar, Dr Fuhrer continued his explorations and discovered some extensive ruins about six miles away that he took to be Kapilavastu.

On 23 December 1897 the Allahabad *Pioneer* published an exclusive that was carried by the international press reporting two great linked discoveries: the birthplace of the Buddha at Lumbini and the ruins at Kapilavastu where the Buddha had spent his childhood. Fuhrer's findings at Kapilavastu were later discredited and its exact location was subject to controversy till relatively recently. But there is no doubt about the importance of Lumbini. Final confirmation was provided in 2013 when archaeologists discovered the remains of a timber shrine at the base of the Maya Devi temple dated to the $6^{th}$ century BC.

## Buddha Gaya

The temple at Buddha Gaya, where the Lord Buddha attained enlightenment, has attracted Western scholars since the late 18$^{th}$ century. One of the earliest was Charles Wilkins who translated the temple inscriptions. Francis Buchanan's discoveries at the site have already been mentioned (*vide supra*). General Cunningham visited the temple in 1861 and ordered immediate excavation of the area around it. The work was assigned to Major Mead. A trench was dug in front of the brick archway revealing many carved model stupas. He enlarged the trench to trace the walls of what turned out to be the lower sections of four small single-cell shrines. In one he found a colossal Buddha on an inscribed pedestal with its head broken off. There was also a bronze bell and a part of a bronze ornament. About 10 yards from the south-west of the temple, the trench that was dug revealed a broken pillar and a Buddhist railing. He found traces of the same railing on the northern and southern sides of the temple.

In January 1877 the King of Burma sent three Burmese to repair the temple. Having obtained permission from the Hindu Mahant, they zealously got on with the work. Later in the year the Government of Bengal asked Rajendralala Mitra, the renowned Indian antiquarian, to visit the site and report on what was going on. He spent three weeks at the site and collected a large amount of information on the site and the temple, made sketches and took photographs and later published a book on Buddha Gaya under the orders of the Government. He was deeply disturbed at the activities of the Burmese. In the course of building new walls, they had demolished ancient remains and many of the antiquities had been swept away. The damage was extensive and, worse still, there was no record of what the site looked like beforehand.

The Bengal Government decided to undertake the restorations themselves and assigned C A Mills to the task. He was asked to work closely with the Collector of Gaya and Mitra. There was some uncertainty whether the considerable costs should be borne by the Bengal Government, the Indian Government or if the King of Burma should be asked to contribute. The matter was referred to Cunningham, who decided that the Government of India should meet the costs. He also suggested that the King of Burma could be asked to contribute towards new buildings, such as residences for monks, but that these should be built quite detached from the objects of worship to prevent disputes between the Buddhists and Hindus.

Cunningham visited the site in 1879 in order to assess the condition of the temple. Signs of the haphazard activities of the Burmese were everywhere. A number of votive stupas had been thrown down. Fortunately, the Burmese had not dug down deeply enough to affect the earlier structural phases of the temple. Cunningham reported to the Bengal Government that urgent repairs were needed. In 1880, Sir Ashley Eden appointed Belgar to supervise the repairs at Buddha Gaya. Belgar started the same year and his excavations uncovered the complex early history of the temple. Among the most dramatic discoveries were the vestiges of an older Asokan temple, fragments of railings and the old vajrasana throne. Several structures were uncovered including a large monastery to the north. Votive stupas and sculptures from different ages were found in profusion. Eventually there were disagreements between Belgar and Cole how much restoration should take place while repairing the building.

Fig 4 - Buddha Gaya

The restoration of the Mahabodhi temple was one of the major works of conservation completed during Cunningham's tenure as Director-General (Figure 4). In his monograph on the History of the Maha-Bodhi Temple, Anagarika Dharmapala writes that: 'The thanks of the Buddhists are due to the enlightened British Government for having restored their central shrine'. On a marble slab over the main doorway leading to adytum of the temple, the following inscription used to stand: 'This ancient temple of the Maha-Bodhi, erected on the holy spot where Prince Sakya Sinha became BUDDHA was repaired by the British Government under the orders of Sir Ashley Eden, Lieutenant-Governor of Bengal, A D 1880'. Cunningham was dragged into the dispute between Belgar and Cole, but the dispute between the archaeologists and architectural scholars was soon to be dwarfed by the bitter dispute between the Buddhists and Hindus for the custody of the site.

At the time of the arrival of the British, a Hindu Mahant was administering the site. During the six centuries following the Islamic conquest, the site had become more and more ruinous. At the end of the 16th century a Hindu ascetic came and settled near the temple and founded a monastery of the Hindu sect of Girs. About the year 1727 the then Mahant of the monastery received by royal farman from the Moghul Emperor Muhammad Shah the grant of the village of Taradih, where the ruins of the temple stood, thus acquiring possession of the site. Though the fabric of the site had been restored by Cunningham and others, several visitors in the late 19th century were disturbed at the lack of reverence shown at the site. In 1886, Sir Edwin Arnold, who had published the epic poem *The Light of Asia* and had retired as the editor of the Daily Telegraph, made an extensive tour of India and visited Sarnath and Buddha Gaya. Arnold's poem was one of the first popular accounts of the life of the Buddha and was greeted with universal acclaim. At Buddha Gaya, he was disturbed to find the Mahant performing Hindu rituals and a large number of pieces of ancient relics of carved stone inscribed with Sanskrit lying around. He wrote to Ven. Weligama Sri Sumangala in Panadura and informed him that he had formulated a proposal that Buddha Gaya and other Buddhist sites should be transferred to Buddhist guardians.

Following his visit to India, Arnold came to Sri Lanka bringing with him some leaves from the sacred Bo tree. These were greatly prized by the Sinhalese Buddhists. The leaf presented to the temple at Kandy was placed in a casket of precious metal and made the centre of a weekly service. Arnold describes how: 'talking to the gentle and learned priests at Panadura, particularly my dear and wise friend Sri Weligama, I gave utterance to the suggestion that the temple and its appurtenances ought to be, and might be, by amicable arrangements with the Hindoo College and by the favour of the Queen's government, placed in the hands of a representative committee of the Buddhist nations'.

I think there never was an idea which took root and spread so far and fast as that thrown out thus in that sunny temple court at Panadura, amid the waving taliputs. Like those tropical plants which can almost be seen to grow, the suggestion quickly became a universal aspiration, first in Ceylon and next in other Buddhist countries'.

Arnold's initial efforts were to write to the Governor of Ceylon, Sir

Arthur Gordon, the Lieutenant-Governors of Bengal and Madras and General Cunningham who all gave their support. He approached the Secretary State for India, Lord Cross. 'Do you wish, Lord Cross', he asked, 'to have four hundred millions of Eastern peoples blessing your name night and day, and to be forever remembered in Asia, like Alexander or Asoka, or Akbar the Great?' 'God bless my soul' replied the Minister 'how is that to be done'? He repeated the facts and the Minister promised to consult the Council and write to the Viceroy. In due time Lord Lansdowne replied that the idea was legitimate and beneficial, and that so long as no religious ill-feeling was aroused, and no pecuniary grant asked from the Indian treasury, the Calcutta Government would be inclined to favour any friendly negotiations.

When the Anagarika Dharmapala visited the site in 1891, he found that some of the Buddhist statues were being included in the Hindu pantheon. Some images of the Buddha and Bodisatvas had clothes put on them. Others were in a neglected state in the garden close to rubbish. In May of that year he and Sir Edwin Arnold founded the Mahabodhi Society with the aim to 'make known to all nations the sublime teachings of the Arya Dharma of Buddha Sakya Muni, and to rescue, restore and re-establish as the religious centre of the movement, the holy place Buddha Gaya, where our Lord attained supreme wisdom'.

The situation at Buddha Gaya came to the attention of the Viceroy, Lord Curzon, who decided to visit the site. Prior to his visit, Curzon had satisfied himself that the Buddhist claims were just and he had 'resolved ..... to question the Mahant on these matters'. During his visit Curzon apparently asked the Mahant how it was that Hindu worship in a Buddhist site could be justified. The Mahant replied that the Buddha was a form of Vishnu. The Mahant's reply did not change Curzon's convictions that the temple, by right, belonged to the Buddhists and he left with his convictions unchanged. Having reviewed the legal history of the place, he saw that the proprietary rights of the place had never been directly addressed in the appropriate arena.

Till 1901, Buddhists had no adequate quarters at Buddha Gaya but in the October of that year, the Collector of Gaya, C E A Oldham, acquired a plot of land to the west of the Burmese Rest House and, with funds the Anagarika had raised in Burma and Ceylon, a beautiful Dharmasala was erected and entrusted to the District Board of Gaya. A plaque inscribed with following text was placed in the Dharmasala: 'This Rest House was built for the use of visitors (especially Buddhists) in the year of the Buddha 2445 (1901) by the Gaya District Board, during the Chairmanship of Mr C E A W Oldham when Sir John Woodburn was the Lieutenant-Governor of Bengal, the Buddhists of Ceylon and Burma contributing Rs 15,000 through the Anagarika Dharmapala, General Secretary, Maha Bodhi Society, for the construction thereof. This tablet has been placed here by the Maha Bodhi Society in grateful acknowledgement of the assistance given. May all attain happiness'.

The Anagarika toured the world to get international support for the Buddhist cause. He first tried to persuade the Mahant to donate the Buddha Gaya site to the Buddhists without any success. He them tried, with the support of the colonial authorities to persuade the Mahant to sell the site. A large sum was collected from the Buddhists of Sri Lanka for this endeavour. The Mahant refused. Finally he tried to assert a legal claim to the site. The litigation was prolonged. It went from Court to Court but finally the High Court decided against the Buddhists. Though the case was lost, the international campaign brought the question of Buddhist shrines in India to the notice of the world and a favourable opinion was created in India and elsewhere. The Anagarika then devoted his energies towards the spread of Buddhism in India. If India became Buddhist minded, the Holy Shrines would naturally come into the hands of the Buddhists. After many years of patient negotiations, agreement was reached between the Indian authorities and the Mahabodhi Society in 1949 on the management of the site.

The Anagarika had a complex relationship with the British. He decried western influence in Sri Lanka, especially regarding drinking alcohol and eating beef and he, no doubt, felt that the authorities in India could have helped the Buddhists more in relation ongoing difficulties at Buddha Gaya. He, nevertheless, appreciated the British role in the re-establishment of Buddhism in India. In a paper on the subject in 1921, he wrote: 'Brahmanical priestcraft and Islamic fanaticism have done their work of destruction, and today, both are alive but with no potency to galvanise a moribund people. Both Brahmanism and Islam had failed within the last thousand years, since the disappearance of the noble religion of the Tathagata to ameliorate the masses. Sunk in ignorance and indescribable poverty millions upon millions of India's people were under the shade of a poisonous fatalism without any hope of progress. Western science and the spirit of democracy, twin sisters born of enlightenment, and of experience gained by the devastating world war, are the beacon lights showing the way to a shore of safety and progress. Under the enlightened administration of British statesmen India is slowly moving onwards, and at this crisis it is the duty of the followers of the Blessed one to re-enter their long lost home, and begin again the great work started by the Blessed One'.

## Sarnath

Sarnath is one of the holiest sites for Buddhists where the Lord Buddha first preached the Dharmachakra Sutta and peoples of the world first heard the four noble truths and the noble eightfold path. Emperor Asoka came on pilgrimage to Sarnath around 250 BC and raised several monuments including the Dharmarajika Stupa and the Dhamek Stupa. Another monument was the monolith pillar surmounted by the magnificent lion capital. The lion capital is now the emblem of modern India. The lion capital was crowned by a grand Dharmachakra symbolising the Supreme wheel of the Doctrine which the Buddha had set in motion at Sarnath. This wheel forms the central part of India's national flag.

When Kanishka ascended the throne in 78 AD, India entered a new phase of religious and artistic activity and a number of new temples and viharas were added at Sarnath. A colossal Bodhisattva image in red sandstone was constructed. During the Gupta age ($4^{th}$ – $6^{th}$ centuries) the main shrine was enlarged and the Dhamek Stupa was encased with carved stone. The famous seated Buddha statue was added. Fa-Xian visited Sarnath around 400 AD and saw four stupas and four monasteries. After his visit the shrines at Sarnath were considerably damaged by invasions of white Huns from the north. Evidence for this was obtained by General Cunningham who discovered a large collection of statues packed in a very small room, which he believed had been hidden away during one of these invasions. Under the patronage of Harsha (600 AD), the last Buddhist Emperor, the site was restored. Hiuen Tsang, who visited the site in 638 AD saw the Dharmarajika and Dhamek stupas and the Asoka pillar. Sarnath was ravaged by Mahmud Ghanzi in 1017 AD but was restored during the Pala dynasty. The buildings were in a good state during the first half of the $12^{th}$ century during the reign of the Buddhist Queen, Kumaradevi.

The site was probably finally destroyed by Muizzuddin Muhammad bin Sam when he sacked Benares in 1193. The conditions of the remains clearly show that the final destruction was accompanied by plunder and fire. Sarnath remained deserted and neglected for the next 600 years. Even the existence of such a holy place was unknown.

The existence of Sarnath came to the notice of the British in tragic circumstances. In 1794, Jagat Singh, the Diwan of Benares, dismantled the Dharmarajika Stupa which was still standing to provide building material for a housing colony. While dismantling the stupa, one of the workmen found a green marble relic casket inside a sandstone box containing human bones, pearls, gold leaves and other jewels. These relics of the Buddha which had been enshrined in the stupa by Asoka were thrown into the Ganges by Jahat Singh. This act of vandalism was recorded by Mr Jonathan Duncan, Commissioner of Benares, who published a report in 'Asiatic Researches' and attracted public attention to the site. The first British explorations were carried out by Colonel C Mackenzie in 1815 and the sculptures found by him are in the Indian Museum in Kolkata.

General Cunningham excavated the site in 1835-36. The cost of the work was borne by himself, James Prinsep and some others. The operations were fairly intensive and of longer duration than any of his subsequent operations. The Dhamek Stupa was opened but the work was slow because it involved removing, one by one, large pieces of stone, secured to each other by iron cramps. Inside the stupa he found a stone slab inscribed with Buddhist inscriptions and he rediscovered the stone box mentioned above. He explored a monastery and temple north of the Dharmarajika Stupa and discovered a large collection of images and bas-reliefs which are also in the Indian Museum.

Major Markham Kittoe, Government Archaeological Engineer, undertook excavations at the site from 1851-2 and exposed a number of stupas around the Dhamekh Stupa. His work also revealed a quadrangular building north of the Jain Temple which he thought was a hospital but was in fact a monastery. While clearing another monastery to the west, he fell ill and died. The work at the site was carried on by several others and in 1877 Mr Rivett-Carnac discovered a Buddha image. Mr F C Oertel, then Executive Engineer of Benares Division, undertook excavations in 1904-05. He exposed the main shrine and discovered the Asoka pillar and the

Fig 5 - (A) Sarnath-Lion capital of Asoka (B) Sarnath-Dhamek Stupa

magnificent lion capital, a galaxy of stupas around it and large number of sculptures and inscriptions. It is interesting to note that India's national emblem – the Asoka lion capital containing the chakra wheel which is at the centre of the national flag- was discovered at Sarnath in 1904 (Figure 5).

In 1907 Sir John Marshall assisted by Dr Sten Konow undertook further excavations both in the northern and southern areas of the site. In the northern area they unearthed three monastic buildings of the late Kushana period and in the southern area around the Dharmarajika Stupa, they brought to light numerous small stupas and shrines. In 1914 further excavations were undertaken by H Hargreaves and Daya Ram Sahni, the then Superintendent Hindu and Buddhist Monuments. They continued the excavations for five consecutive field seasons.

The Museum of Archaeology was proposed by Sir John Marshall during the excavations in 1904-05. The designs were prepared by James Ransome, then Consultant Architect of the Government of India. The building is modelled on the usual type of an ancient Buddhist monastery, several examples of which had been unearthed in Sarnath.

In November 1935, a ceremony took place at Sarnath during which Mr J F Blakiston, Director-General of Archaeology in India, on behalf of the Viceroy, the Earl of Willingdon, presented relics of the Buddha to the

Maha Bodhi Society. During Mr Blakiston's address, he recounted the role the Survey had played in the reintroduction of Buddhism in India: 'It gives me great pleasure to present to you on behalf of the Government of India the sacred relics found at Mirpur Khas in Sind in 1910 by the late Mr H Cousens of the Archaeological Department. On two previous occasions relics from two other sites in different provinces namely, Taxila in the Punjab and Nagarjunikonda in the Madras Presidency, were presented to you by Government through my predecessor for enshrining at the Mulagandhakuthi Vihara at Sarnath. As you are all aware, the spread of the Buddhist faith from the land of its birth has been phenomenal. During the millennium that followed the Master's death, it became the predominant faith almost throughout India, and had already reached the distant regions of Ceylon, Tibet, Siam, China, Japan, Mongolia, Afghanistan and Central Asia. In most of the regions the light of Buddhism continues to shine since it was introduced but in India, itself, interest in Buddhism has ebbed and the work of following up the path of the ancient development of this faith in various parts of the country has fallen to the Archaeological Survey of India since the latter part of the 19$^{th}$ century. The Survey can lay claim to having restored, to some extent, the ancient fame of places like Sarnath and Bodh Gaya, Sravasti and Kasia, Sanchi and Bharut, Nalanda and Paharpur, Taxila and Peshawar, Amaravati and Nagarjunikonda. Some of the relics discovered during earlier explorations being claimed by Burma and Ceylon, countries closely associated with India, in which Buddhism is still the dominant faith, were presented to them by the Government of India. With the renewal of interest in Buddhism in India, thanks to the activities of Societies like the Maha Bodhi Society, it is but natural that the relics of the Master and the Great Teachers who followed him, so dear to the faith and so reverentially consecrated in the centuries of its rise should be preserved in India itself, and particularly to be re-assembled at the Holy Centre where the doctrine first saw the light of day'.

## Kushinagara

Kushinagara was the place of the parinabbana of the Buddha. Emperor Asoka visited the site and built stupas and pillars. Both Chinese pilgrims, Fa-Xian and Hiuen-Tsang paid homage at the site. The latter describes 'a great brick Vihara, in which is the figure of the Nirvana of the Thathagata. He is lying with his head to the north (facing west) as if asleep'. He also noted a stupa over the site of the Buddha's cremation. Kushinagara continued to be a living site of pilgrimage till the 12$^{th}$ century. Thereafter it appears to have been deserted and fell into oblivion.

In modern times, the ruins were first visited by Dr Hamilton Buchanan in 1811-12 but he did not realise its significance. In 1854, the great Sanskrit scholar, H H Wilson casually alluded to the identity of Kasia, a near-by village, with ancient Kushinagara. It was left to the far-sighted Cunningham, who visited the site in 1861-2, to identify the ruins as the place of Buddha's parinibbana. Subsequently in 1876, Cunningham's assistant, A C L Carlleyle carried out extensive excavations of the site. He completely exposed the main stupa and discovered at its front, the famous Nirvana statue of the Buddha, buried in the debris of the ruins of an oblong shrine. He also discovered a statue of the Buddha, broken into two pieces, at the shrine locally called Marthakuar which he repaired and restored.

Further excavations around the Main Stupa and the Nirvana Temple in 1904-07 were undertaken by J Ph Vogel and in 1910-12 by Hiranand Shastri. J Ph Vogel excavated a stupa close to the stupa and temple of the dying Buddha. There were other small stupas of various shapes and sizes and a monastery. He found a seal of the Mahaparinirvana monastery, thus confirming the identification of the site. In 1910, a small circular brick chamber was discovered containing copper vessel. On the mouth of the vessel was a copper plate, inscribed on which was the text of the Nidana sutta. The excavations also yielded datable remains which indicated that the site was in occupation till the 12$^{th}$ century. These finds included a clay seal with the representation of the coffin of the Buddha in between two Sal trees with the legend 'mahaparinirvana' and 'bhikshu-sangha'.

## Sravasti

Even in the time of the Buddha, Sravasti was an active centre of Buddhism. It was here that the merchant Anathapindada built in the garden of Prince Jeta, which he had purchased for a fabulous price in gold, a magnificent vihara and other shrines and monasteries. Out of the forty-five rainy seasons during his Buddhahood, the Buddha spent twenty-five, twenty-four continuously at Sravasti. The majority of the sermons delivered by the Buddha were delivered at the Jetavana Monastery. The site continued to expand as a Buddhist shrine after his parinibbana. Emperor Asoka visited the site as part of his pilgrimage and he erected two pillars on the left and right sides of the eastern gate of the monastery. He is also said to have built a stupa to enshrine the relics of the Buddha adjoining the well where the Buddha used to draw water and the place where he used to walk and preach.

During Kushana rule (1st–2nd centuries AD) new shrines and images were erected. A colossal statue from this period can be seen at the Indian Museum in Kolkata. When Fa-Xian visited Sravasti in 407 AD, the city was decaying and the stupas and vihara were in ruins. Some of the Buddhist edifices had been replaced with Brahamanical temples. However, the Jetavana Monastery was in excellent condition and still in use. By the time Hiuen-Tsang visited the site in 637-38 AD the site was in ruins, the Jetavana Monastery had decayed and there was no one living it. There was a subsequent revival at Sravasti during the reign the Gahandavala kings. One of whom, Mahandapala, founded a vihara in 1119 AD. Another, Govindachandra (1129-30 AD) gifted six villages to the monks at Sravasti. This liberal gift was at the request of his Buddhist Queen, Kumaradevi, who had also been a benefactor at Sarnath. After the 12th century the site fell into oblivion and completely forgotten.

Sravasti, which is located at modern Sahet-Mahet, was one of the several Buddhist sites identified by General Cunningham in his 1862-63 tour. He excavated the Jogini-baria mound and discovered the site of the Jetavana monastery. He traced a number of structures including walls and wells. The opening of the brick stupa yielded no relics but a colossal Buddha figure was discovered with an inscription from the 1st century bearing the name Sravasti thus confirming the identification. He revisited the site in 1876 and there was a very thorough operation to excavate the Jetavana monastery. His report contains a map of Jetavana showing all the ruined buildings. He cleared away the jungle as much as possible. He hastened the progress by offering rewards to the diggers if they found statues or structures. Excavations were made in twenty mounds. Ten yielded remains of temples, five of stupas and five others of dwelling houses or mounds previously dug up for bricks.

Further excavations were undertaken by Vogel, Marshall and Daya Ram Sahni during the 1907-08 and the 1910-11 seasons. In the 1907-08 season, Vogel conducted large scale excavations at Sravasti employing 1600 labourers of whom 230 cleared the jungle. Mahet was a crescent shape city site possessing high ramparts and a number of gates. Here he found two circular basements of two stupas from the Kushan period. At Sahet, D R Sahni provided further identification of the Jetavana monastery based on a copperplate inscription from the period of King Govendachandra dated 23 June 1130 AD which recorded the grant of six villages to the 'community of Buddhist friars.... residing in the great convent of the holy Jetavana'. In the 1910-11 season, Marshall made further large scale clearances of the Jetavana complex and showed Sravasti to be an important centre of the Mathura school of art.

## Nalanda

Nalanda was one of the main centres of Buddhist learning and its University flourished from the 4th to the 12th centuries with several thousand students attending from India and abroad. With endowments from several monarchs, the University contained many imposing buildings. The site has earlier connections for Buddhists as the Buddha visited Nalanda several times and delivered some important sermons. Moreover, Sariputta and Moggalana were born nearby. The site was destroyed during the fatal invasion of Bakhtiar Khilji towards the end of the 12th century. It is said that most of the monks were killed and the libraries set on fire. It took six months to burn. For centuries it lay in ruins, unknown and unidentified.

Francis Buchanan visited the ruins which lay near the village of Bargaon in 1811-12 but did not realise its significance. General Cunningham identified the site during his 1861 tour. He judged that the major buildings were built after 410 AD as they were not described by Fa-Xian. However, they were later described graphically by Hiuen-Tsang and this enabled Cunningham to identify Nalanda and other ruins such as the temple of Baladitya. Hiuen-Tsang spent several years at Nalanda. He wrote that: 'the whole establishment is surrounded by a brick wall. One gate opens into the great college from which are separated eight other halls standing in the middle. The richly adorned towers and fairy-like turrets and pointed hill-tops are congregated together'. Cunningham wrote that the village of Bargaon surrounded by ancient tanks and mounds possessed 'finer and more numerous specimens of culture' than any other place he had visited. He discovered two inscriptions which read 'the place itself is called Nalanda'.

The major excavations were undertaken during John Marshall's period initially by J A Page in the 1920s and later by M H Kuraishi and G C

Fig 6 - Nalanda, Main Temple

Chandra in the 1930s (Figure 6). The excavations at the complex showed a row of four temples on the western side in a north-south arrangement. The main temple lay at the south-west corner had evidently been rebuilt several times. Eight monasteries formed a straight row to the east of the temples while two others formed an oblique corner in the southeast. The monasteries were quadrangles with cloistered cells on the inside. The excavations yielded a very large number of inscribed seals, sculptures and bronze images. The seals read 'The monastery of the noble community of the monks of Nalanda'. The discovery of pieces of charcoal and pieces of charred wooden beams strengthened the conclusion that the monasteries were destroyed by a great fire.

## Sanchi

Sanchi, unlike the other sites of Buddhist pilgrimage, was not visited by the Buddha. The site is not mentioned by the Chinese pilgrims. The monuments at Sanchi were constructed by the Emperor Asoka and are the most magnificent and perfect examples of Buddhist architecture in India. It is thought that Arahant Mahinda stayed at the site on his way to Sri Lanka. The Asokan Stupa was extensively damaged by the opponents of Buddhism following the break-up of the Mauryan Empire in 185 BC but was soon rebuilt by devotees. The elaborately carved four gateways were added in the first century BC. An addition was made to the Great Stupa in

450 AD when four seated images of the Buddha, under a pillarded canopy, were installed facing the four entrances. Around the great Stupa grew a grand complex of stupas, temples, pillars and monasteries which flourished till the 12$^{th}$ century. From the 13$^{th}$ century, the site was deserted and engulfed by jungle.

The site which lay in Bhopal State was discovered by General Taylor in 1818 and the monuments were in a fairly good shape. In 1822, T H Maddock and his assistant T H Johnson visited the site and dug a shaft from top to bottom of Stupa-1 in search of relic boxes and damaged the stupa. In 1851, Captain F C Maisey, who was undertaking archaeological work in Central India and Alexander Cunningham came to Sanchi. They opened up several stupas by digging a single shaft at the exact centre to minimise damage. They found several relic boxes and caskets, including the relics of Sariputta and Moggalana in Stupa-3. These are described in Cunningham's publication *Bhilsa Topes* in 1854. Unfortunately, there is no mention of them filling up the shafts after their investigations.

After the initial investigations, no restorative work was undertaken for several decades till H H Cole became curator of ancient monuments. By this time, the site had been further damaged by local inhabitants and encroaching jungle. Restoration work at the site was begun in 1881 under the supervision of Austin Mears, Superintendent of Public Works. The costs of the restoration were shared between the Imperial Government and Shah Jahan, Begum of Bhopal. Mears cleared the jungle, collected all the carved stones and railing pieces, repaired the stupas. The roots of the trees that had damaged the railings and stupas had to be bored into and destroyed with sulphuric acid. The ground was carefully sloped to prevent waterlogging. The northern gateway was cleaned, the stone pavement exposed, sections of the railings re-erected and several Buddha images restored in their original places. In spite of his efforts, the task of rescuing other crumbling structures – shrines, monasteries and stupas – from vegetation and debris and protecting hundreds of sculptures and inscriptions lying about was left to John Marshall several decades later.

Marshall and his colleagues worked on the site from 1912-19. Their operations had four objectives. Firstly, the whole enclave up to the limits of the surrounding wall, which dated from the later mediaeval epoch, had to be swept clear of jungle. Then, extensive areas to the south, east and north-

Fig 7 - Sanchi

east of the Great Stupa had to be excavated – a task that involved the removal of some millions of cubic feet of debris. Thirdly, the many fallen parts of the buildings had to be pieced together and, as far as possible, restored to their original positions and the buildings themselves strengthened and protected from the ravages of the climate. Fourthly, a museum was built to house the many antiquities that the spade had brought to light and the whole site was beautified by levelling and turfing and planting trees and creepers (Figure 7). A visitor wandering through the courts and chambers of the monastery today would find it difficult to realise that scarcely a vestige of them was visible from the ground before the efforts of the British archaeologists.

## Ajanta Caves

The Ajanta Caves are some of the finest Buddhist caves in India and are unique in that they combine the three best examples of architecture, sculpture and painting. They belong to the period from the 2nd century BC till the 7th century AD. It is thought that the construction work at Ajanta came to a halt in 642 AD when the Chalukyan king was overthrown by a Pallava king, who forcibly removed the skilled workers to work on Hindu temples. This may explain why some of the paintings are unfinished. The Ajanta caves fell into desolation and ruin after Buddhism declined in India. They became covered with natural growth and lay buried in the jungle-clad slopes for more than a thousand years till they were accidentally discovered by a pair of British soldiers out on patrol in the western mountain range. In 1829 the first descriptions of the caves appeared in the *Transactions of the Royal Asiatic Society* and in 1843 James Fergusson laid before the same society an authoritative account of the rock-cut temples at Ajanta. As a result of the interest shown by the members of the Society, Major Robert Gill of the Madras Army was asked in 1844 to make copies of the paintings. Major Gill worked on these paintings till 1863 and the copies were sent to museums in London but, unfortunately, most were destroyed in the Crystal Palace fire. In 1872 Sir James Fergusson and James Burgess urged the Indian Government to make further copies. In 1875 the work was entrusted to Mr George Griffiths who undertook the task with the help of students from the Bombay School of Art. He worked on the project till 1885. Some of his paintings are shown in the monumental work *The Paintings of the Buddhist Paintings at Ajanta* (1896). Lady Herringham came to India in 1906 and was so fascinated by the frescoes at Ajanta that she made two further visits. The result of her work with a band of Indian artists was another sumptuous volume entitled *Ajanta Frescoes* (1915). These publications have given the public a clearer idea of the wonder of the frescoes.

The conservation work at Ajanta has been undertaken by the Department of Archaeology of the State of Hyderabad. The passage of time and the inclemencies of weather had decayed the frescoes to such an extent that the painted surface was falling off. In a few cases, the frescoes had been smeared by some injudicious artists with varnish which as the existing dirt had not been removed, gave the paintings a dingy appearance. Two Italian experts worked on the paintings from 1920-22 and restored the frescoes.

By the early part of the 20th century, Buddhist pilgrims and tourists had begun to visit the Buddhist sites in India. In 1907 the Indian Railways Board complied a 'Traveller's Companion' containing brief descriptions of important towns and places of pilgrimage. Its entries for the major Buddhist sites were:

**Budh-Gya** - It is 292 miles from Calcutta and is of great historical and religious interest as being the head-quarters of ancient Buddhism, of which religion the great temple Budh-Gya, 7 miles from the railway station, is now one of the chief remnants. Buddhists are now allowed to remain permanently at Budh-Gya, where there are at present Buddhist monks and where a remarkably beautiful image of the Budh, brought from Japan, is located in the Burmese monastery. The shrines at Gya are now in the hands of the Brahmans and are largely resorted to by pilgrims for shradhs or funeral ceremonies, in consequences of a belief that by performing shradhs at Gya the souls of departed relations are at once transported direct to Vaikuntha, or the Heaven of Vishnu.

**Sarnath** - It is next in sanctity to Budh-Gya. It is three and a half miles north of Benares. Sakya Muni first preached his doctrine here. And some of the ruins probably date from his time (543 BC). The most remarkable, specially known as Dhamek, is a solid dome 93 feet in diameter and 100 feet above the plain. There are two other stupas and remains of many other buildings. The Dhamek tower probably stands on the site of that was erected by Asoka to mark the spot where Budh first preached his doctrine.

**Sanchi** - It is a village in the Bhopal State and is situated 5 miles south of Bhilsa, and within 15 minutes' walk of the hill on which still stands the famous 'Sano Tope', one of the most ancient and interesting Buddhist relics in India. The most ardent archaeologist will find himself amply repaid by a visit to the tope. The country for miles around is studded with Buddhist remains. But only at Sanchi itself are the remains abundant and well preserved. Here may be seen carvings illustrative of Buddhist worship and ritual as they obtained in the days of the celebrated Asoka and are interesting studies. Sanchi is referred to by the Chinese pilgrim Fa Hian in his description of the great Kingdom of 'Sha-chi'.

The edition of The Times on the 18 February 1930 contained the following vivid account of the Buddhist sites in India:

'The Monuments of India – Buddhist Stupas – The buried cities which the excavators' spades are bringing to light in the Sind Valley have a special interest for the archaeologist and race-historian, and may be expected to illuminate some region of darkness in which the antiquity of India's civilization is hidden. But of the standing monuments which primarily interest the tourist, none dates later than about 260 BC, when the great King Asoka carved on rocks and pillars the main precepts of the Buddhist faith. Two of the Asoka pillars are to be seen in Delhi – one in the ruined palace of Feroz Shah, and one on the ridge near Hindu Rao's house. A better pillar, which also bears later Gupta and Moghul inscriptions, rises in the Fort at Allahabad,

The finest specimen of building, however, are the topes (stupas) which mark some spot sacred to Buddha, or were meant to contain some relic of his, the rails which surround these and other holy places, the chaityas or churches, and viharas or monasteries. Far the most impressive group that survives is that at Sanchi in the Bhopal State, on the railway between Bombay and Agra. Topes, rails, monasteries and some later temples are nobly set on a hill commanding wide and beautiful views, and the visitor will indeed be dull of imagination who does not feel the sanctity and grandeur of a place that is almost comparable with the Acropolis. Less impressive than Sanchi, but not less interesting, is the tope at Sarnath, near Banares, which marks the beginning of Buddha's mission as teacher. The work of the Archaeological Department described by Mr Hargreaves on this page, has made the purpose of the several buildings very clear, and an admirable little museum houses some famous pieces of Buddhist sculpture. Holier than either of these in Buddhist eyes is the temple at Buddha Gaya, near by the bodhi-tree where the Buddha attained enlightenment, a lofty pyramid like building said to have been built by a Brahman, in the days of religious tolerance about AD 500 before Buddhism was swept out of India by the Brahmanic revival. The later development of the characteristic Buddhist railing can be studied best at Amraoti and Bherhut, but the best specimens of chaityas are the rock-hewn caves of the Bombay Presidency, of which the most famous are those at Karli, Bedda, Nassik, Ajanta and Ellora. Some of these in plan are curiously like an early Christian church, with a nave, aisle and apse. Karli is architecturally the finest, but the cave pictures at Ajanta have a nobility which the art of painting never again attained in India and from them some of the best Indian artists of today draw inspiration'.

There were a sufficient number of tourists and pilgrims in the 1930s that Indian State Railways were advertising rail tours of the sacred Buddhist sites in India (Figure 8).

Fig 8 - Indian Railways Poster (1938)

In September 1935, Rai Bahadur Daya Ram Sahni, late Director-General of the Archaeological Survey of India, gave a lecture in London on the achievements of the Survey and The Times on the 20th of the month contained the following report: 'The lecturer said that many of the acts of the Buddha early on became favourite subjects with pious Buddhist artists, but no representation of these events earlier than the time of Asoka had survived. The only representation of the career of Buddha so far noticed on an Asokan monument was that of the Edicts of the capital at Sarnath. The Bharut and Sanchi railings, however, bore medallions showing Jataka stories with the master clearly depicted in animal and human form.

During the palmy days of Buddhism, the sacred places were maintained with care and adorned with religious edifices of various kinds. They fell to ruins about the twelfth century AD, and became buried and forgotten until the Archaeological Department took up the task of their exploration and resuscitation. The sites were first identified by that talented pioneer of Indian archaeology, Sir Alexander Cunningham, and how successful he was in that task with the meagre facilities available in his time was apparent from the fact that although some of his identifications were severely criticized and even rejected by the late Dr Vincent Smith, their correctness had now been conclusively established by architectural, sculptural, and epigraphical records brought to light by systematic exploration. Buddhists throughout the world might well be grateful to the Government of India and to Sir John Marshall and other officers of the Department whose researches had enabled the Buddhists to resume their holy pilgrimages which had been interrupted for several centuries'.

## Museums

In addition to restoring historic sites, the British established about one hundred museums in India and Burma. These acted as a focus for research and enabled the general public to better appreciate their culture and heritage including India's Buddhist past. The genesis of the museum movement in India can be traced to the founding of the Asiatic Society of Bengal by Sir William Jones in 1784. By 1796 the Society had to consider how to house the 'curiosities' that had been donated by their members. In 1796 the Society established a museum in Calcutta comprising two sections, one archaeological and ethnological and the other geological and zoological. The museum grew rapidly but by 1836 the Society was financially weak and requested funding from the Government for the maintenance of the museum. The East India Company agreed in 1839 and from time to time they received grants. After protracted negotiations, the Government, itself, decided to house the collections and the Indian Museum was constructed in Calcutta and opened in 1875.

Elsewhere as early as 1819 the Madras Literary Society formed a museum for economic geology in Madras. In 1843 at the request of the Society, the East India Company agreed to form a Central Museum in Madras. The museums in Lucknow and Nagpur were established in 1863 and that at Lahore the following year. The celebration of Queen Victoria's golden jubilee in 1887 ushered in a new era of museum building in India and elsewhere in the Empire. The museums at Jaipur, Udaipur, Rajkot and

Vijayawada are among those that were built for the occasion. But the greatest impetus for the museum movement was the viceroyalty of Lord Curzon whose keen interest was matched by the enthusiasm of Sir John Marshall. The museums at Ajmer, Baripada, Chamba, Jodhpur, Gwalior, Bijapur, Khajuraho and Dacca were established with a space of ten years from 1903. The museums at Malda, Bijapur, Dhar, Peshawar, Pagan, Mandalay and the one in the Taj Mahal at Agra were established at the insistence of Lord Curzon.

In the early stages the nucleus of museum collections was geological and zoological but after the formation of the Archaeological Survey, the place of archaeology in museums came to be felt. Through the indefatigable efforts of General Cunningham the museums came to possess the rich archaeological collections which they pride today. Even before the Survey was established, in 1835-06, Cunningham presented to the Asiatic Society a large collection of Buddhist images of the Gupta period from Sarnath, which now adorn the sculpture gallery of the Indian Museum. As Director-General, Cunningham presented to the Indian Museum several Gandhara Buddhist sculptures and the magnificent Bharhut rail and gateway which are the most valuable treasures of the museum. Similarly, Colonel Colin Mackenzie saved what he could from the Amaravati Stupa which he discovered in 1797 and portions of the rail and carvings form some of the priceless treasures of the Madras Museum. This museum was also fortunate in receiving a fine collection of Gandhara sculptures in the 1880s thanks to the generosity of Major H H Cole.

Some of the major Buddhist sites have their own museums. The Sanchi museum in the Bhopal state was built in 1919 and owes its inception to Sir John Marshall. It contains all the antiquities recovered by him at the site. It was built, furnished and arranged under his personal supervision. It illustrates all the phases of central Indian history from the time of Asoka till 1200 AD. The Nalanda museum was opened in 1917 and contains all the antiquities that could not be preserved *in situ*. These include remarkable sculptures in stone and bronze which represent the Pala art from the medieval period. Other important antiquities are the sealings of the Gupta and Maukhari dynasties and official seals of the Nalanda monastery. The erection of the Sarnath museum in 1904 was at the initiative of Sir John Marshall who conducted excavations at the site for two seasons. The building was designed by James Ransome and the plan is that of an ancient

Buddhist monastery of which Sarnath has yielded many examples, the small cells being replaced by large halls for the exhibits. Standing in a well-planned garden, the building of Chunar stone is worthy of both its setting and the treasures it enshrines. These antiquities represent different phases of Indian art spanning some fourteen centuries. These include Mauryan, Sunga, Andhra, Kushana and early Gupta sculptures, including the Asokan Lion Capital, Mauryan portrait heads, the colossal Bodhisattva of the Mathura school with its carved stone umbrella railings of the Sungha period, inscribed Gupta Buddha images and Mauryan pottery and terra-cottas. There are also other Gupta antiquities and examples of the mediaeval and late periods.

It is evident that Archaeological Survey of India during the British period rediscovered, restored and studied practically all the Buddhist sites in India. Holy places associated with the life of the Buddha were revealed after centuries of oblivion. It is interesting to consider the fundamental factors which facilitated these achievements. Firstly, the country was at peace with an effective central government. It was possible to devote State resources for archaeological research. It is not surprising that many British officials, who were steeped in the Classics and were used to touring the Roman and Greek cities in Europe were fascinated by Pali and Sanskrit and the ancient sites in India. They were from a land where learned societies for the study of arts, culture and natural phenomena were common. Hence it was inevitable that they replicated them in India. The British were also committed to documenting everything they discovered in reports, journals and books. Their spirit of adventure and their ability to endure hardships allowed the early British explorers to discover India's forgotten sites. Many of them were in the Indian Army. That they ruled the neighbouring countries, Burma and Sri Lanka and the documents they discovered there, first alerted them to the existence of the Buddha. They believed in the freedom of religion and rights of minorities. For the first time in nearly a millennium, Buddhists in India could practise their religion freely. Though they were not Buddhists, the British respected the logical basis of Buddhism. These are some of the factors which enabled Buddhism to re-emerge and India to regain its Buddhist heritage.

# 3
# Legacy in Sri Lanka

Following the end of the golden era, at the beginning of the fourteenth century, till the eighteenth century Sri Lanka passed through periods of unrest punctuated by intervals of peace. One glorious interval was the reign of Parakramabahu-VI in the middle of the fifteenth century. The two centuries following his death constitute a dark chapter in Sri Lanka's history. The coastal region was in the hands of foreigners and the interior comprised of several kingdoms and areas controlled by petty chieftains. There was no paramount central authority. As far as Buddhism was concerned, there was a deterioration in the morale and the discipline of the Sangha and powerful pressure from Hinduism. Buddhism suffered greatly during the rule of the Portuguese. Temples and monasteries were razed to the ground and their priceless treasures looted; libraries were burned and monks were put to death. The few bhikkhus who survived fled inland and carried with them some of the books. The Dutch were more tolerant of indigenous religions than the Portuguese. They helped the Kandyan Buddhists maintain contact with the rest of South-East Asia and re-establish *upasampada* and the purity and the strength of the Sangha by enabling Buddhist monks to travel to other countries. However, they introduced Protestant Christianity and religious missionaries who were very active. The schools they established functioned both as church and school. Births and marriages had to be registered in church. Only Christians could hold even minor government posts. Some Buddhist, termed Government Christians, pretended to be Protestants to obtain jobs. There was a resurgence of Buddhism in the Kandyan kingdom in the mid-18$^{th}$ century during the reign of Sri Rajasinghe-II under the inspiration of Ven. Saranankara Sangharaja.

## Buddhist Revival

The position of the Buddhists initially improved with the arrival of the British as the Kandyan Convention provided that the Buddhist religion should be protected and maintained by the Government. All religious persecutions ceased. The British recognised religious tolerance though the provision imposed by the Dutch in relation to registration of births and marriages remained for a long time. When people saw that conformity to Christianity was not insisted upon by the new government, the number of Government Christians began to fall off rapidly and more than halved between 1801 and 1810. People who hitherto had professed their religion with some amount of secrecy found that this was no longer necessary. Buddhist ideals were practised again openly with renewed vigour. No sooner did the British occupy the maritime provinces than the freedom to ordain monks which had been restored in Kandy, was extended throughout the island leading to a revival of religious activities. In the early years, the Governor took part in the annual Tooth ceremony. He continued to appoint Nayaka Theras and the officers in charge of the Dalanda Maligava (Temple of the Tooth). He enforced the services rendered at religious festivals by those who held Maligava and devala lands and gave grants towards their expenses out of the revenue of royal villages. But this created resentment from the church and the Governor's involvement was eventually discontinued. There were no restrictions on the Buddhists, themselves, partaking in their religious activities. However, when the Nilames (temple custodians) were deprived of their judicial powers, they found it difficult to exact services from their tenants. Furthermore, the British officials did not show the veneration to the monks that they were used to. These were some of the factors that led to the 1818 rebellion.

The Colonial Authorities did continue to appoint Chief Bhikkhus in both the Kandyan Provinces and the Maritime Districts. However, in 1847, owing to strong pressure from the Church, the Colonial Government decided to discontinue the practice of appointing senior monks and vested all the powers to the Bhikkhus themselves. The connection between the State and the internal affairs of the Sangha ceased to exist and resulted in considerable disquiet among the Buddhists. There were also continuing disputes between low country Buddhist activists and the Government on one side and those who controlled wealthy Kandyan viharas on the other as to the proper use of revenues generated from their extensive land holdings. This issue of Buddhist temporalities dogged the relationship between the Colonial Authorities and the Buddhist clergy for many years. After the 1848 rebellion a compromise was reached that the Bhikkhus would appoint their own Theras but the Government would issue an instrument recognising the title. They also granted crown lands yielding an annual income of £350 in place of the annual payments towards the cost of the Dalada Maligava rites.

Greater difficulties were caused by the activity of Protestant Missionaries. While Catholic Missionaries mainly ministered to their own congregations, the Protestant Missionary Societies took active measures for propagating their religion with the moral support of Government officials. Firstly, the missionaries were in a position to recommend men for office and honours. Secondly, they started numerous schools, partly with public funds. These schools were active centres for teaching Christianity. Thirdly, they adopted methods of ridiculing Buddhism. Lectures, books and pamphlets were issued in large numbers. These activities gradually affected the people. The public began to lose their love and enthusiasm for Buddhism. Some were easily tempted to discard Buddhism and embrace Christianity. Buddhism became unfashionable and there was a danger that it would disappear from the island in a few decades.

Fortunately, there was a turnaround in the fortunes of the Buddhists in the second half of the 19th century. After the 1848 rebellion the Colonial Office became less rigid and evangelical than before. It conceded that it had an obligation to supervise how legal functions affected the religion. There was a succession of Governors who were sympathetic to Buddhists. In 1876, Gregory received numerous complaints about the misuse of vihara and devala properties and appointed a Commission of three Government Agents to look into the problem. They reported that Government intervention was needed to stop the scandalous misappropriation of temple revenues and widespread corruption and systematic fraud. Gregory proposed to vest the control of Buddhist temporalities in three Commissioners appointed by the Governor. But he was unable to obtain general agreement. Gregory made two symbolic gestures to support Buddhism. Firstly, there was a contribution from the State for the repair of the Ruwanveli Dagaba; this was followed by a gift of two lamps for the Dalada Maligava (Temple of the Tooth). Governor Gordon looked at the issue of Buddhist temporalities again in 1886 and proposed that the control of Buddhist properties in each district should be transferred to the control of a committee of Buddhist laymen elected by Buddhist Bhikkhus and laymen of the area and empowering it to elect the trustees of the viharas and devales. This system, too, proved too complicated to administer as the general level of education among the laity was insufficient. Further changes were made to address the issue in 1907.

Most importantly of all, Buddhists took matters into their own hands. Individual Bhikkhus began to enter public discussions to counter missionary propaganda. The most notable was Ven. Migettuwatte Gunananda who took part in the debates at Panadura. He started lecturing against Christian indoctrination and his speeches roused the enthusiasm of the Buddhists. He was a talented writer and a good speaker and as an orator he was pre-eminent. Buddhist laymen who had acquired great wealth by taking part in new enterprises introduced into the country by the British began to establish printing presses, publish tracts and form societies for Buddhist propaganda.

The arrival of Colonel Olcott in 1880 transformed the situation. He, at once, placed his finger on the weak points that were undermining the national religion. He urged the Buddhists, if they wanted to restore confidence in the national religion to meet their opponents on their own grounds. In the first place he pointed out that the colonial government was neutral in regard to religious matters and the people should give up their belief that the government favoured any particular religion or that people who sought high office should become Christians. If any particular official did so, they acted wrongly without the sanction of the government and were liable for correction. In the second place he said that the Christian Mission bodies were establishing schools with public funds and these grants from the government were open at all communities and it was the fault of the Buddhists themselves if they did not take up these opportunities to establish their own schools. Thirdly, he pointed out that public opinion was an important factor for any government and Buddhists should not be passive sufferers nursing their grievances in silence, but should assert themselves in all public matters.

The Buddhists had a well-established infrastructure at the time. Practically every village in the island had its own Buddhist temple and Bhikkhus. Amongst these were some of outstanding ability and learning including, Ven. Hikkaduwa Sri Sumangala, Ven. Weligama Sri Sumangala and Ven. Dhammarama. The activities indicated by Colonel Olcott had their strong support and Buddhists, at last thoroughly awakened, started to work in earnest. Olcott realised that the Buddhists themselves were woefully ignorant of the fundamentals of their religion. After considerable labour, the Colonel compiled a 'Buddhist Catechism' which rapidly became best seller. Olcott also asked the Governor Gordon to make Vesak Day a national holiday and to end the need for Buddhists to register their marriages in Christian churches. The Governor readily agreed.

To co-ordinate these efforts, Olcott founded the Colombo Buddhist Theosophical Society (BTS) in June 1880. Several British residents played a prominent role in the Society. They included C W Leadbeater who had earlier been a Christian Minister. He founded the English Buddhist School which eventually became Ananda College. He served as the first Principal of Ananda. He wrote to the Press effectively meeting criticisms levelled at the Society. He founded the English supplement of the *Sarasavi Sandaresa* under the name of *The Buddhist.* J Bowles Daly was a journalist who had worked for the *Daily Telegraph.* He travelled throughout the island and roused up the people to great enthusiasm. Mahinda College, Galle, and Dharmaraja College, Kandy, owe much to him. F L Woodward rendered valuable service to both education and religion. His name was long remembered by the pupils of Mahinda College, Galle.

Under the guidance of Colonel Olcott and with the support of the all the bhikkhus, the people rose to the occasion. Propaganda was started, newspapers, books, pamphlets and leaflets were issued in their thousands and lectures were arranged throughout the island. Within a short time, schools were opened. The operation of these schools was modelled on the Christian schools, though their curriculum was very different. At the time of Olcott's arrival, there were only three Buddhists schools in the island. Now the number of schools increased rapidly. The BTS, itself, founded 56 schools by 1892, 260 by 1925 and 420 by 1940. The Government grant for Buddhist schools increased from Rs 84 in 1888 to Rs 27,430 in 1898 and to Rs 74,740 in 1909. A very large number of schools were also founded by other societies and private individuals. The government was tardy in recognising these schools but these difficulties were overcome and the revival of Buddhism spread with a rapidity which was unexpected and gained unprecedented success. Several British Governors aided the expansion of Buddhist schools. Governors, Sir Graeme Thompson and Sir

Herbert Stanley and Acting Governor Sir Murchison Fletcher all gave land for Ananda and Nalanda Colleges. In 1922 Thompson laid a foundation stone for an extension at Ananda College and he gifted the land on which Nalanda College was built.

In a chapter on Buddhism, Past and Present in the monumental tome *Twentieth Century Impressions of Ceylon* (1907) Anagarika Dharmapala noted the considerable improvement in the general environment for Buddhists: 'The present spiritual condition of the Buddhist population in Ceylon is causing anxiety to the orthodox followers of Buddha. There is very little inclination shown by either the clergy or the laity to observe strictly the precepts of the 'Noble Eightfold Path'. As regards, materialistic development, however, the Buddhist community in the island has, since 1862, been showing its ability to march with the times. Printing presses, newspapers and journals devoted to the religion have been established, and colleges for teaching Pali, Sanskrit, classical Sinhalese, Ayurvedic medicine, astrological mathematics, and kindred subjects have been founded. The Vidyodaya College was founded in 1873.

The present generation of Buddhists in the Maritime provinces of the island are showing remarkable activity in opening elementary schools for children. Several English colleges and about 400 Buddhist vernacular schools under Buddhist management have been established, while about 7900 Bhikkhus are keeping up the ancient traditions, and new temples are being built in various parts of the island. Ancient historic dagabas (monuments) in the ruined city of Anuradhapura, in the North-Central Province of Ceylon, and in Magama, in the hill country, another of the ancient capitals of Lanka (Ceylon) are being restored by Buddhist contributions'.

The revival continued though it halted temporarily during the 1915 riots. In a paper presented at a conference on *Some Living Religions of the Empire* in 1924, the eminent Buddhist nationalist, W A de Silva, included a section on 'Open Revival under British Government' and noted: 'There are at the present time about 7,000 Buddhist Bhikkhus in the island, and nearly 400 educational establishments for them, where they receive instruction in Pali and Buddhist literature. Practically 99 per cent of Bhikkhus possess a knowledge of Pali and higher literature of Buddhism'. The author clearly recognised the significant role played by the colonial authorities in the revival of the religion. In his *History of Buddhism in Ceylon* (1931), Dr De Silva went on to say: 'Today within fifty years of this revival the disabilities which the Buddhists had to face have disappeared. A Conscience Clause as regards religious teaching has been introduced in all schools as a condition of receipt of government grants. Offices and honours do not go according to religious beliefs. The voice of Buddhists is a strong in public affairs as the voice of any other religious persuasion. The controversies between Buddhists and Christians have ceased. There is a marked mutual respect and tolerance between all religious workers. The Buddhists and Christians join in social and welfare work and religious peace is evident throughout the country..... Buddhist religious activity is alive today as it was at any time in the history of the island'.

Though the Christian missionaries caused difficulties for Buddhists, in some respects they benefitted the country. As D B Jayatilaka conceded in a speech to the Young Men's Buddhist Association in 1899: 'At the very outset let me frankly admit that in this respect Christian missionaries have rendered much service to the country. They were more or less pioneers of modern education in Ceylon. Let us not be blind to the benefits they have conferred on the Sinhalese through their schools and let us give them every credit for the good they have done in offering the people an opportunity for intellectual improvement at a time when theirs was the only agency existing for the purpose. I would give them due meed of praise and admiration for the energy and devotion which many of them have shown in the work of education'.

In addition to the revival of their religion, Buddhists in Sri Lanka benefitted during the British period in two further ways. The first was the restoration of the ancient cities and the second, the study of sacred texts.

## Restoration of Ancient Cities

Anuradhapura was the ancient capital of Sri Lanka from the 2$^{nd}$ century BC till the end of the 10$^{th}$ century when the capital moved to Polonnaruwa. Both cities were abandoned in the middle of the 13$^{th}$ century following invasions from the north. By the time the British arrived both cities had been abandoned for centuries, in a ruinous state and ensnared by jungle. The earliest Briton to discover the ancient cities was a Lieutenant Fagan who came across the ruins in the early part of the 19$^{th}$ century and wrote an account in *The Ceylon Gazette* in October 1820. Several other British

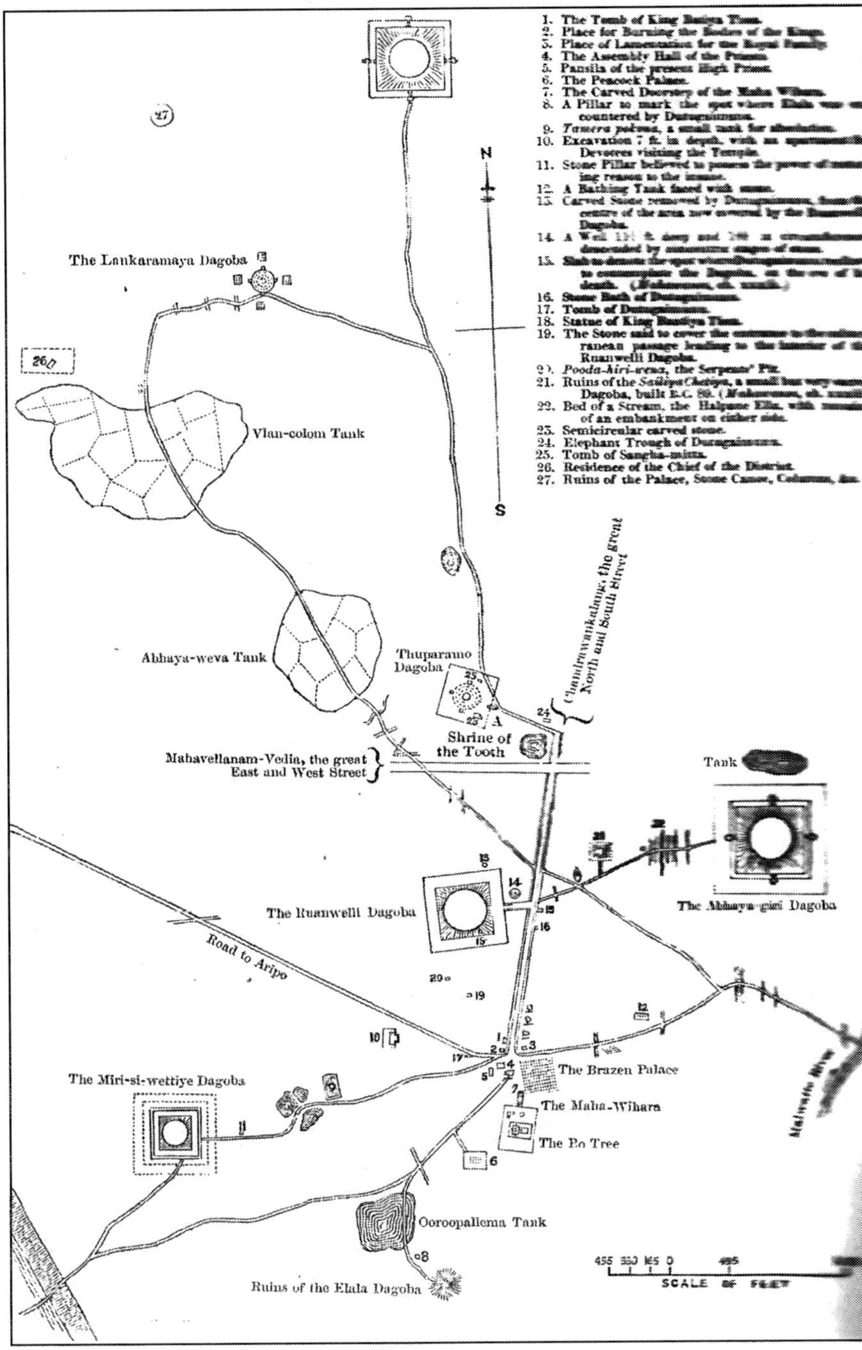


Fig 9 - Major Skinner's map of Anuradhapura (1832)

officials subsequently visited the ruins, Major Skinner while constructing roads in 1831 (Figure 9) and Major Forbes who gave a detailed account of the sites in his book *Eleven Years in Ceylon* (1840). They noted that individual monks had been trying to clear the jungle around the dagabas. In 1868, during the governorship of Sir Hercules Robinson, seven years after the establishment of the Archaeological Survey of India, the Ceylon Government appointed a Commission to obtain information regarding the ancient architectural works of Ceylon. In 1871, an excellent series of photographs of the principal ancient structures in Anuradhapura and Polonnaruwa was taken by Mr Lawton. In 1873, under directions from Governor Gregory, a complete survey of all that was known about ancient Anuradhapura was made by John Capper and the heights and measurements of the larger dagabas were determined. By 1877, detailed plans and drawings to scale of the more important ruins at Anuradhapura had been undertaken by Mr Smither. Between 1875 and 1879 a search for ancient inscriptions had been instituted. An analysis of the collections of inscriptions was published by Professor C Goldschmidt and E Muller. At the same time Maha Mudaliyar L de Zoysa was authorised to visit the main Buddhist temples in order to examine and report other manuscripts of historical importance in their custody.

Early efforts to restore the sites started on a small-scale at the same time. In 1870, Rhys Davids who was a member of the Archaeological Commission was given leave by Governor Robinson to conduct research at Polonnaruwa from September to October 1870. Given his interest in the Ancient Cities, he was appointed Assistant Government Agent for Anuradhapura. After his appointment as Governor, Sir William Gregory gave Rhys Davids precise instructions for clearing the trees and roots from the areas around the dagabas, making detailed plans of the important edifices and collecting inscribed stones and other large objects which might be sent to the Colombo Museum. Gregory was close to Ven. Naranwita Sumarasara Unnanse, who himself was endeavouring to restore Ruwanveliseya. Gregory gave him Rs 1000 to help his efforts. In a personal testimonial in 1876 Gregory wrote: 'The vigour displayed by Naranwita Samarasara Unnanse deserves every encouragement, and I trust it will be appreciated by his countrymen. I myself have contributed to this restoration, not looking at it as a religious work, but as the conservation of a great national monument characteristic of the best period of Sinhalese art and identified with one of the most powerful and enlightened kings who have ever ruled this country'.

On February 09, 1884, at a General Meeting of the Royal Asiatic Society Ceylon Branch (RASCB), at which Sir W H Gregory was present, the Governor, Sir Arthur Gordon, said to the members present: 'I should like some archaeological work undertaken and I understand from the information I have received that it would cost no large sum to complete the excavation of the very interesting dagaba (Mirisawetiya) in the immediate vicinity of the prison at Anuradhapura. There have already been uncovered most interesting sculptures, and I believe the sides of the wall presented sculptures of some kind. Besides the sculptures, in the opinion of those competent to judge, many interesting remains will be found. I would propose, therefore, that the Members of the Society should subscribe for this purpose. I am willing to head the list myself as funds are wanted'. In response to this appeal, a sum of about Rs 1,000 was subscribed by the Society and excavations commenced under the supervision of Mr S M Burrows (Ceylon Civil Service). This meeting initiated the systematic exploration and restoration of Sri Lanka's ancient sites and it was fitting that Gregory and Gordon, who were both so committed to the study of Sri Lanka's culture and heritage were present.

During the years 1884-86 Burrows undertook work relating to monuments and other antiquities at Anuradhapura and Polonnaruwa. He cleared the thick jungle around the Anuradhapura ruins. He unearthed a new building with a stone canopy which has been termed 'Burrows Pavillion'. At Polonnaruwa many buildings were cleared of vegetation including the Thuparama, Hetadage, Sat-Mahal-Prasadaya and the Rankot and Kiri dagabas. Burrows also tunnelled into the Demala-Maha-Seya and revealed wall paintings, some of which had earlier been copied by A Murray. In addition, old roads were restored and new roads constructed. Schemes for further excavations were drawn up. A local museum was started to house 'curios' and preserve the sculptures and paintings which had survived destruction from the ravages of time and the rapacious hands of local vandals. The costs were kept to a minimum by employing prison labour. With the benefit of his experiences Burrows wrote; *The Buried Cities of Ceylon* in 1885, the earliest guide books of the ruined cities.

Governor Gordon also authorised considerable government expenditure for repairs to the great Abhayagiriya dagaba. A section of the square 'tee', the box or tower at the summit which supported the crowning pinnacle, had fallen down. In a letter to the Secretary of State for the Colonies, written from Anuradhapura on 11 August 1886, he applied for retrospective sanction for this work, which he set in hand immediately given its precarious state:

'It appeared to me that the preservation of a national monument of such historical and archaeological interest as this structure (only inferior to the pyramids in mass and elevation) was well worth the attention of this government, and seeing the danger to the pinnacle to be imminent and immediate action to be necessary, unless the dagaba was to be allowed to perish, or greatly increased expenditure incurred in undertaking repairs at a later period. I authorized the immediate commencement of such repairs to the base of the 'tee' (as it is called) as were necessary to ensure its continued support of the terminating pinnacle which rises to the height of nearly 300 feet. Of these repairs which are progressing satisfactorily, I have now to ask for your Lordship's approval. They have been made on an estimate by the Provincial Engineer, Mr A Murray, amounting to Rs 3,000; out of this sum Rs 1,500 will be paid by the Buddhist Committee of this place, from scanty funds in their hands. The remaining Rs 1,500 is not, I think, an unreasonable contribution from the government towards the preservation of so remarkable and ancient a building, more especially when it is remembered that the estates once supporting it have passed into the hands of the crown'.

The work was carried out by successive Provincial Engineers under the keen supervision of Ievers, the Government Agent. As well as repairing the summit, a shaft was driven into the centre as local tradition had claimed that valuable Buddhist books had been buried there. All that was found were scattered objects including beads, pottery and a small crystal dagaba. The work at Abhayagiriya during this time provoked opposition from two different directions. Some criticised the Government that money should not be spent on religious monuments as this compromised their impartiality between all religious faiths. The tunnelling caused outrage to some Buddhists. The Governor refused to be drawn on the implication of Government support for Buddhism but rested his case on the duty of the Government to maintain important historical monuments irrespective of their purpose. On the other hand, Mr Ievers' tunnelling, although he had obtained the prior permission of 'a leading and intelligent Buddhist Chief of the Central Province, of the High Priest of Adam's Peak and of the High Priest of the Bo Tree' was opposed by a number of individuals who formed a Abhayagiriya Defence Committee, was discontinued. Ievers had, in any case, agreed that all the finds would be replaced and this was done under the supervision of the High Priest of Adam's Peak. These events illustrate the difficulties archaeologists face when excavating sacred sites.

The years leading up to the establishment of the Archaeological Survey show the ever rising degree of interest in the historical and archaeological remains of Sri Lanka by individuals, the Royal Asiatic Society Ceylon Branch and by successive Governors. Governors Sir William Gregory and Sir Arthur Gordon were notable in this regard.

## Archaeological Survey of Ceylon – H C P Bell era

The need to restore these spectacular sites prompted the Ceylon Government to establish The Archaeological Survey of Ceylon. They realised that work on this scale required Government support. A regular vote for archaeological purposes was inserted in the supply bill in 1890 and introduced to the Council by the Governor, Sir Arthur Gordon, with the following message: 'It is proposed to make some systematic examination of the interesting remains at Sigiri and to commence on a modest scale, before the rapidly disappearing monuments of the past have altogether perished, a species of archaeological survey resembling that carried on in India. The scope of the survey, as succinctly defined by Lord Canning contemplated: An accurate description – illustrated by plans, measurements, drawings and photographs, and by copies of inscriptions – of such remains, as most deserve notice, with the history of them so far as it may be traceable, and a record of the traditions that are retained regarding them'.

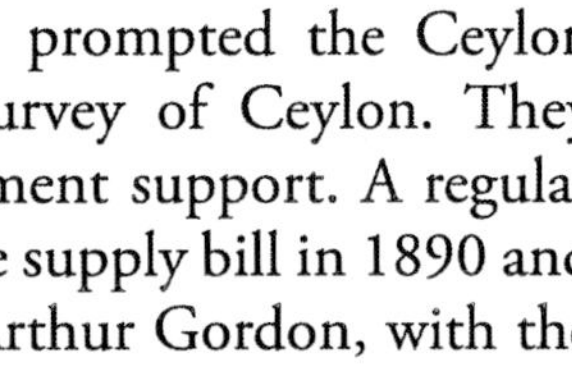


Fig 10 - Sri Lankan postage stamp commemorating H C P Bell

Consequently, H C P Bell was appointed Archaeological Commissioner in February 1890 (Figure 10). He commenced his career in Sri Lanka as Writer to the Ceylon Civil Service in 1873 and rose up the ranks and became Acting Assistant Government Agent in Kalutara in 1879. He was a committed member of the Ceylon Branch of the Royal Asiatic Society and became its Secretary in 1880. He visited the Maldives and produced several publications about the islands for the Society. Though Gordon had proposed that Sigiriya should be the first objective of systematic study, Bell, who had been Acting District Judge at Kegalle since 1888, suggested to Gordon that he should start with the district of Kegalle which he said contained several sites of considerable historic interest. Gordon agreed.

After working in Kegalle till July 1890, he published a report in 1892. It was a landmark in antiquarian studies in the island. It was arranged under four headings. The Introduction dealt with the historical geography of the Kegalle district. Part I (Historical) recorded as much as history Bell had been able to glean from records, chiefly from the 15$^{th}$ century onwards. Part II (Antiquarian) summed up the characteristic forms of architecture and temple adornment of the district and gave detailed descriptions both of ancient sites and of the more important viharas, dewales, and kovils of each Korale and Pathuwa. Part III (Epigraphical) described all the stone inscriptions and copper plate or palm-leaf grants discovered in the course of his research. The final part contained the Appendices which gave miscellaneous information about the District. The report constituted the first fruits of the Archaeological Survey of Ceylon.

In June 1890 Bell started working at Anuradhapura and the following ten years were probably the happiest and most interesting of his life. During this time he produced seven detailed progress reports on Anuradhapura, three interim reports on Sigiriya and commenced work at Polonnaruwa. He toured the whole of the North-Central Province visiting, recording and restoring all the ancient sites and many of the great waterworks of the district.

Life is seldom without some travails. He complained that his pay as 'Special Commissioner detached for Archaeological research' was less than that as District Judge. He wrote to Sir Arthur Gordon saying he did not know how he could manage and even threatened to give up. Luckily for Bell, his friend Ievers, Government Agent (GA) for Anuradhapura, wrote to Gordon explaining away Bell's imprudent letter. Bell then wrote to the new Governor, Sir Arthur Havelock on the same matter and, though they still refused to increase his salary, withdrew his threat of resignation. It was not the Government's intention to make the job permanent and, indeed, he was taken away from Anuradhapura and stationed in Kalutara as District Judge for eight months in 1894. From the first, Bell felt that the post should carry the title 'Archaeological Commissioner'. He returned to his archaeological work in 1895 and was officially appointed Archaeological Commissioner with a salary of Rs 9600. In 1897 the post was back-dated from 1890. Bell was delighted and wrote: 'The die is cast and I am to cling to my Archaeology dry bones. I am eccentric enough to sincerely rejoice'.

Bell proceeded to Anuradhapura on 7th July 1890 in accordance with the directions of the Governor Sir Arthur Gordon. The annual vote for this year was Rs 10,000. Bell initially employed a labour force of twenty Sinhalese and Tamil labourers but this was increased to thirty during the year. He had no regular clerk or interpreter but the GA helped by sparing a Kachcheri clerk to work out of office hours. Mr D M de Z Wickramasinghe, Assistant Librarian at the Colombo Museum, was seconded to help him with translating inscriptions. His plan for Anuradhapura was laid out at the beginning of his annual report for 1890 as follows:

'As a first step, it was decided to utilize the small labour force at Anuradhapura on a thorough and systematic exploration of the jungle between the defined limits (eg. the Inner and Outer circular roads) with the preliminary object of ascertaining definitely what ruins exist above ground. The excavations of likely sites can then follow with more economy of time, labour and expense than under the irregular and spasmodic efforts hitherto employed. Such methodical exploration, if slow and barren of frequent startling discoveries, is the only sure means of satisfactorily carrying out that 'complete survey and excavations of Anuradhapura' contemplated by the Ceylon Government'.

The work was inevitably slow, as even areas which had once been cleared were soon again overgrown and impenetrable. His reports frequently referred to the dense, prickly and exasperating nature of the undergrowth which had to be cleared. The weather also caused difficulties. The north-east monsoon in 1891 was very severe and all the low ground in Anuradhapura became standing pools and fieldwork suffered. Bell, himself, was seriously ill for five months between August 1892 and January 1893. The main excavations at Anuradhapura are listed in Bell's *Summary of Operations 1890-1900* as follows:

| | |
|---|---|
| Vijayarama ruins | 1890-1891 |
| Abhayagiri ruins | 1890-1893 |
| Pankuliya ruins | 1891-1892 |
| Kiribat Vihara | 1892-1893 |

*Contd...*

| | |
|---|---|
| Tamil ruins | 1892-1893 |
| Jetawama ruins | 1890-1894 |
| Toluvila ruins | 1893-1895 |
| Mayurapada Pirivena | 1894 |
| Ruins on Ayton Rd | 1894 |
| Sela Chaitiya | 1895 |
| Shrine on Kurunegala Rd | 1895 |
| Thuparama-Ruwanveli ruins | 1895-1900 |
| Mullegala ruins | 1896 |
| Puliyankulam ruins | 1896-1900 |
| Elala Sohana | 1896 1900 |
| Shrine on Y road | 1898 |
| Citadel | 1897-1898 |

In his report to the Thirteenth Congress of Orientalists in 1902, Wickremasinghe picked out as the most important of the excavations at Anuradhapura, those of Abhayagiriya, Vijayarama, Pankuliya and Toluvila. The excavations around the Abhayagiriya (Jetawanarama) Dagaba began around September 1890 and were gradually extended to unearth a large monastic complex eventually clearing debris around the dagaba and excavating four entrance porches, altars and chapels. In one of his progress reports, Bell reflected what the edifice must have looked like originally: 'In the days of its glory it must have presented a magnificent appearance externally, with its milk-white basement and stairs of quartz glittering in the sunlight; whilst within, after dark, the chaste beauty of the carvings of the shrine would have been immeasurably enhanced by lights coruscating from columns mica-cased'. The discovery of 'Buddhist Railing' – a stone post with three rails attached, in two pieces was an exceptional discovery, a find which he reported to Gregory on June 1891 'I am not a little proud'. This was the first structure of which restoration was attempted.

The Vijayarama monastery, which had partly been cleared by Burrows, was the first of the complete monastic complexes excavated by Bell. He reported on it in considerable detail in several progress reports. He summarised his findings in the Annual report for 1891 as follows: 'By the more complete felling of the jungle which hid the greater portion of the Vijayarama ruins, and by systematic excavation, the ruined buildings and their co-relation leave no room for doubt that here existed a typical *sangharama*, or Buddhist establishment, perfect in itself, with its shrines and meeting halls, its priestly residences, bath-house, store rooms, ponds, etc.'. In the debris around the basement of the dagaba, thirteen copper plates of great importance were found, cleaned and translated. This enabled the age of the construction of the dagaba to be fixed with fair approximation.

The Pankuliya ruins had been visited by Ievers in 1887. He had seen a sedent Buddha which had fallen forward but the site was too deeply buried in jungle to be examined. After excavation Bell reported; 'The image measures approximately 7ft from head to seat, and is as usual carved from quartz. The pose of the broken arms and hand shows that this sedent Buddha was sculptured in the *asirawara-mudra*, or attitude of blessing. As since raised and replaced with hands fitted on, the figure is undoubtedly the finest of the large Buddhas yet discovered at Anuradhapura'. Another monastic site fully excavated was the ruins at Toluvila. Here, in 1890 another sedent Buddha was found. Bell was equally impressed with this statue: 'In mere size it yields to the seated Buddha in the outer circle which measures 7ft 6in in height and 7ft across the knees. But in other respects it surpasses all three statues near the Jetawanarama. The wonderful sharpness and depth of features, the softness of expression, the symmetry and repose of the body, give the image a *tout ensemble* which contrasts markedly with the solid 'figure-head' appearance so characteristic of these Buddhas in stone. The eye-lids, under-lips, and ears are carved with a life-like reality not reached in the other Buddhas already known. The nose is chipped, but so slightly as to be practically unnoticeable from the front; the fingers are somewhat worn, and there are a few cracks. With these slight blemishes, the Sage sits as serenely contemplative as when votaries flocked to worship and make their offerings upon his altar'.

Bell started his excavations at the rock fortress of Sigiriya in 1894. The rock had been abandoned since the 5th century AD and was rediscovered by Major Forbes of the Indian Army in 1831. The earliest known ascent was made in 1853 by Messrs. Adams and Bayley (Ceylon Civil Service). In 1875 the Pali scholar Rhys Davids observed the frescoes with a telescope. In 1889 Mr Alick Murray was asked by Governor Gordon to reach the frescoes. The resident chiefs and the local population refused to disturb the rock as they believed it was inhabited by demons. So three Tamil stone-cutters had to be brought to bore holes on the rock face one above the other in which iron jumpers were secured with cement. To these wooden staging was lashed. This enabled the lightest man to climb. But after a while he declared that it was impossible to ascend any higher. However, after he was allowed three days for fasting and prayer he thought he might succeed and indeed he did. When the pocket containing the frescoes was reached, the floor was too steep for anyone to stand or sit. Iron stanchions were let into the floor and a strong trestle made to secure them and a platform was placed on the framework. Mr Murray had to lie on the platform on his back from dawn to dusk for a week copying the frescoes. There was a sheer drop of 160ft below him. Mr Murray's tracings caused much interest and Bell was asked excavate the site.

Bell surveyed the area around the rock in 1894 but did not climb it till 1895. He first reached the top by means of jungle wood ladders and six inch grooves cut in the rock. Once up, iron ladders and an iron rail were fixed so that constant ascent and descent was possible. The top was found to be covered with a forest of trees and dense undergrowth, neck high, so a gang of Sinhalese workers was engaged to burn them down. Excavating necessitated removing earth to a depth of five to twenty feet and when the whole area was cleared, the plan of the long lost buildings was easily seen, virtually as perfect as first laid out. The working conditions were difficult. During the first fortnight the workers were attacked by swarms of bees and their nests had to be burnt. The greatest trial was the heat of the sun from which there was no shelter. The whole day had to be spent aloft as too much time would have been spent coming down and up for a meal.

Fig 11 - D A L Perera painting frescoes at Sigiriya

Fortunately, in 1896 a big cistern was discovered which provided drinking water.

Accompanying Bell was his draughtsman D A L Perera and both were keen to photograph the frescoes in the two caves. There was insufficient space in the two caves to take photographs so a chair was lowered from the summit with the photographer sitting with the camera. But as the chair swayed in the wind, the photographs were blurred. Hence Mr Perera decided to do oil paintings of the frescoes (Figure 11). Thirteen of the pictures were painted from the floor of the cave but for the others it was necessary to construct a cantilever of jungle timber firmly lashed to a stout iron cramp let into the rock floor. To the extremity of this projection was tied a rough cage of poles. In these extraordinary, dangerous and eerie open-air studios, Mr Perera spent nineteen weeks painting on canvas a complete set of the 22 frescoes which were first painted 1400 years ago. The frescoes were painted in 1896-7. However, the intensity of the sunlight temporarily affected Mr Perera's eyesight and he had to take a period of rest while receiving special treatment in Colombo.

In 1898 Bell summarised the early work carried out at Sigiriya as follows: 'In brief, the three previous seasons had witnessed the first clearing of most of the forest undergrowth overlaying the site of the extensive

Fig 12 - Ruwanveli Dagaba during restoration

ancient city, the completion of a topographical survey of the whole area with the *vil-bemma*; the thorough excavation from end to end of the citadel which stood on the summit of Sigiri-gala and of the two staircase approaches to the gallery along its western face; the securing facsimile copies in oils of virtually all of the paintings, which have survived to this day in the Rock pockets, and the carrying out of other minor but essential work with the view to the conservation of the ruins of Sigiriya'.

In 1900 excavations at Anuradhapura were continued at the same sites as in 1899 namely at Ruanweli Ruins, Elana Sohona and Puliyankulama Ruins (Figure 12). The first operations at Polonnaruwa were undertaken between May and September. The site, since its rediscovery in 1820, was thoroughly photographed by Lawton in 1870 when it was partially cleared. Some further clearing was done upon the order of Sir Arthur Gordon by the Disawe of Tamankaduwa in 1885-86. The Durawa was worked under the direction of Mr S M Burrows. Initial work clearing the forest and scrub jungle from the ruins situated on the promontory overlooking the tank. These comprised: the 'Council Chamber', the 'Audience Hall', the 'Pavilion' and the 'Mausoleum'.

The work of the Archaeological Survey progressed steadily during 1901-03 clearing and pushing back the jungle at Anuradhapura, Polonnaruwa and Sigiriya. The area between Thuparama and Ruwanveli Dagabas was excavated between 1900 and 1903 and there was major excavation work at the Mirisavetiya Dagaba from 1902 to 1903. At Sigiriya, the Citadel on the summit, the terraces at its base and the caves and 'islands' within the ancient city were weeded out and cleared. The restoration of the gallery reached the foot of the old limestone steps. The wide gap in the gallery between the end of the iron bridge and the existing steps had to be built up. The cramped lower steps had to be broadened out to provide a wide staircase. A concrete bed was laid over the rough sloping floor of the fresco pockets, an iron hand-rail fixed along its edge and wire netting stretched along the whole mouth of the cavern.

During 1904-06, the work in Anuradhapura involved clearing jungle, thinning out trees, removing spoil from previous excavations to make it easier to view the ruined monasteries etc. The excavations at Vessagiriya, begun in 1906 by John Still, who had been appointed Assistant to the Archaeological Commissioner in 1902, continued until 1911. Mr D M de

Z Wickramasinghe left the Archaeological Survey to undertake further research in Europe. Since 1898, he had been working on epigraphical material supplied by Bell to publish, under the authority of the Ceylon Government, the journal *Epigraphia Zeylancia* to translate the ancient inscriptions of Ceylon. The first issue was published in 1904 and its contents comprised records in Brahmi lipi from Vessagiriya, three Sinhalese slab inscriptions from the 10$^{th}$ century, a Sanskrit on a slab from Jetawanarama ruins. The excavations of the Mirisavetiya area were rounded off. During 1907-10, field operations were undertaken Anuradhapura, Sigiriya and Polonnaruwa. At Anuradhapura, large amounts spoil and earth were removed to fully expose large areas containing groups of ruined buildings. Bell's work in his final years was largely concerned with excavations around the Jetanawarama Dagaba and the restoration of its summit. A great amount of progress was made at Polonnaruwa, where the digging took place over several sites, including the magnificent Vihare, the Demala-Maha Seya, the furthest north of all known ruins of any importance. Mr John Still, Assistant Commissioner had to leave in 1907 after serving 5 years due to ill health. His duties were taken over by Draughtsmen D A L Perera and W M Fernando and another Draughtsman W J Fernando was appointed.

Excavation is only the beginning of the work of an archaeologist; what is excavated must be conserved. In the early Annual Reports conservation referred to the purchase of land around the major monuments so that they could be protected from treasure seekers or those wanting to use the stones for building material. In 1891 the following areas in Anuradhapura were set apart for conservation by the Crown: Abhayagiriya, Elana Sohona, Jetawanarama and Lankarama, Kiribat Vihara, Mirisavetiya, moated site below Nuwara-vewa, Pankuliya, Pulitankulam, the Shrine on Y road, Toluvila, and Vijayarama. Eleven acres Vessagiriya were so designated in 1903. These areas were marked out with concrete posts topped with the royal crown. In 1914 the areas surveyed in Polonnaruwa were declared property of the Crown as an Archaeological Reserve. The whole area within the fortifications at Sigiriya had been declared a conservation area in 1898.

In 1890 F H M Corbett, Joint Secretary of the RASCB with Bell, wrote to the Colonial Secretary suggesting that Ceylon might adopt the same rules for the protection of objects of archaeological interest in force in India. Bell supported the measure and suggested that it should cover 'antiquities or anything of value hidden in the earth, or anything affixed thereto'. He also suggested increasing the reward offered for the find. The Governor, Sir Arthur Havelock, accepted Bell's suggestion and the amended Ordinance was duly passed in 1891. He also drafted a circular which the Government issued as a General Circular that placed the responsibility for reporting discoveries of archaeological interest on the Government Agents. In spite of this, there were further instances of damage by treasure hunters and Bell persuaded the Government in 1900 to enact *An Ordinance for Better Preservation of the Antiquities of the Island.* This was concerned with establishing a policy of safeguarding the whole cultural heritage of the Island rather than merely regulating the reporting of finds. All moveable antiquities were declared Crown property; permission of the government was required before any excavation was allowed to take place. The export of antiquities was prohibited without express leave and this was not granted if any museum in Ceylon wished to acquire the object. A penalty was laid down for the wilful damaging of antiquities. In his last report he reaffirmed the Government's policy of leaving antiquities where they were found whenever possible.

In Ceylon, there were particular problems facing the archaeologist in that, as most of the monuments were religious in origin, some were still in use for religious ceremonies. In 1869 the Temple Lands Commission had been handed over responsibility for the 'Eight Sacred Sites' at Anuradhapura to the Buddhist Committee of the Atamasthana. These sites comprised: Jetawanaramaya, Lankaramaya, Thuparamaya, Abhayagiriya, Lowa-maha-paya (Brazen palace), Bodinwahanse (Sacred Bo Tree enclosure), Mirisavetiya and Ruwanveli. Some Buddhists opposed any excavations taking place particularly in and around dagabas. Walisinha Harischandra, the Secretary of the Maha Bodhi Society, was particularly active in this regard.

After the extension of the railway to Anuradhapura in 1905, it was much easier for both tourists and pilgrims to visit the ruined cities. Bell wasn't entirely happy with the increasing popularity of pilgrimages to Anuradhapura and wrote: 'To those lovers of antiquity undisturbed who can remember the days, not long ago, when it was possible to approach all the ruins at Anuradhapura without having one's eyes and nose offended by incongruous sights and smells – makeshift tables (mostly packing cases), curry and rice. Kevun, plantains, bread, tea, coloured drinks – any cheap comestibles, in fact except spirituous liquor – at one point openly provided under the very shadow of the saintly Buddha, sitting *saxeus* in silent sorrowful reproof, as it were, at such desecration, these ancient sites may well seem to echo the cry, *Ichabod, Ichabod*'. Bell was not alone in being concerned at the lack of reverence shown at the sites. In 1903 there were disturbances as pilgrims objected to the sale of liquor and meat products near the holy sites. Bell also had disputes with the Public Works Department. He accused them of damaging archaeological sites by blasting slab rock when building roads near the Vessagiriya at Anuradhapura. The Government officials were inclined to discount some of his complaints, remarking that: 'Mr Bell is apt to be a little hysterical...This is a storm in a tea cup. Mr Bell is morbidly sensitive when his ruins are in any way affected'.

The actual restorations of the monuments, the re-setting of fallen stones and bricks or even the complete dismantlement of ruins and rebuilding them were not one of the objects of the Archaeological Survey. The only major restoration work authorised by the Government up to that time had been the work on the Abhayagiriya Dagaba begun by Sir Arthur Gordon and that on Mirisavetiya, largely funded by a Siamese Prince. An independent operation on the Ruwanveli Dagaba had been started by the monk Naranvita Unnanse with the support of Governor Gregory. Bell was very much of the opinion that the restorations should be undertaken by the Buddhist Committee of the Atamasthana. In the case of the Mirisavetiya Dagaba, Bell was critical of the architectural merits of the restoration.

In December 1896 the whole of the west front of the tee of the Abhayagiriya Dagaba collapsed and this raised fundamental questions as to the method of reconstruction being employed. There followed a series of investigations on the restorations of the two dagabas. The first was conducted by F A Cooper, the Director of Public Works for Ceylon. He concluded that the collapse at Abhayagiriya was inevitable and nothing could be done to prevent it but that, with certain modifications, the work could continue at Mirisavetiya. The matter was now taken up by the Royal Asiatic Society (RAS) in London who wrote to the Governor, Sir West Ridgeway, saying: 'The RAS is deeply impressed with the opinion that such a structure cannot be allowed to perish or become a mere pile of ruins through neglect without discredit to the Government both of this country and the colony'. Ridgeway wrote back to say that the RAS may rest assured that the Government was not indifferent or lukewarm in the cause of the preservation of National Monuments at Anuradhapura or elsewhere and it had and had continued to expend a considerable amounts of money to that end but that the Government had to be guided by professional advisers as to the possibility and the possibility within reasonable limits of expenditure of restoration and preservation. Gordon, who had now become Lord Stanmore and had been behind the RAS letter, was not satisfied and wrote to Sir Arthur Havelock, who had succeeded him as Governor and was then the Governor of Madras, for assistance. Havelock sent G Harris of the Public Works Department (P.W.D) in Madras. Having surveyed the dagabas, Harris agreed with Cooper that the expense and complexity of repairing the tee at Abhayagiriya was prohibitive. Stanmore was still dissatisfied and arranged for another expert, F O Oertel, a Fellow of the Royal Institute of British Architects, of the Indian P.W.D. to have a look. He concluded that there was a method of stabilising the tee but the cost would exceed Rs 10,000, which was huge amount at the time.

Neither the RAS nor the Buddhist community were willing to meet this cost and after a debate in the Legislative Council, it was decided to set aside Rs 2,800 for the partial restoration of Abhayagiriya. In subsequent years a smaller amount was given for the 'general upkeep' of the dagabas. Oertel had pointed out that greater sums must be set aside for the preservation of the historic monuments and that they should be handed over to the P.W.D. who should do what may be needed for their conservation in consultation with the Archaeological Commissioner. The Government accepted this part of his report and the special grant for restoration was gradually raised to Rs 21,875 by 1910. With this money Bell was able to carry through some extensive restoration work in his last years particularly at Polonnaruwa, Yapuhuwa and the dagabas at Anuradhapura. He offered that the Archaeological Survey should carry out a modified plan to Abhayagiriya to stabilise the tee and this was accepted by the Government. Bell gave full details of the work in his reports for 1910 to 1912. The work was hazardous and some fearless blacksmiths from Lenadora, which was 50 miles away, and had worked at Sigiriya had to be called. Bell now felt that enough had been done to stabilise the tee and the pinnacle and that the fuller restoration should be left to the Antamasthana Committee and the Buddhist Community generally.

Though Bell visited the Polonnaruwa ruins briefly in 1893 and again in photographing the site in 1897, the major excavations at the site did not start till 1900 with the increased archaeological funding. The main areas excavated were summarised by him in the *Ceylon Manual* of 1912-13 as follows:

| | |
|---|---|
| 1900-1901 | Ruins on Promontory |
| 1902 | Hindu Dewales |
| 1903 | Ruins on raised quadrangle near Topaweva |
| 1904 | Raja Maligawa |
| 1906 | Potgul Vihare Monastery and Siva Dewale 2 |
| 1907 | Gal Vihara and Siva Dewale 1 |
| 1908 | Hindu Dewales |
| 1909 | Demala Maha Seya |
| 1910-1911 | Jetawanarama Vihara, Kiribat Vihara |

When these areas were excavated in 1901, Bell found a large pokuna, fed from the Topaweva by a sluice, with an ornamental shower bath at one end. In his 1901 Report he drew attention to the fact that modern excavation had confirmed details of the *Mahavansa*. Later in 1901, Bell recorded the discovery, which was made by John Still, further north, of the Lotus Bath which the *Mahavansa* had spoken of as being among the many pokuna constructed by the great Parakramabahu. Of the Watadage, or Circular Image House, which he excavated in 1903, Bell states simply that 'it is unrivalled as the most beautiful specimen of Buddhist stone architecture

Fig 13 - Watadage before restoration

Fig 14 - Watadage after restoration

existing in Ceylon'. In the first year the ruin was cleared of debris, the outer slab wall temporarily reset and one of the four Buddha images, which had been found round the central dagaba, pierced together and replaced facing the north entrance. As soon as he had secured a grant for further restoration, major work was undertaken in 1904 and after a pause in 1905, resumed in 1906. The south-west quadrant was completed in 1907; it proved to be the most damaged of the four and the stairs had to be completely dismantled and rebuilt. In 1907 drains were made to run from the centre though the surrounding brick wall to prevent damage from standing water and in 1911 the final repairs to the wall and the central dagaba were completed. Bell felt that he had left 'this magnificent granite ruin as well conserved as possible' (Figure 13 and 14).

The Nissanka-Lata-Mandapaya (Nissanka's Flower-Scroll Hall) was restored in 1910-11 and 1911-12. Bell described it as 'that gem of airy sculpture in granite' and that the restoration was 'far the most difficult piece of renewal of battered and grossly maltreated stonework the Archaeological Survey had ever undertaken'. The whole ruin had to be dismantled and rebuilt. In the first year, the post and rail fence were pierced together and reset with the plinth and dado of the basement. Some of the pieces of the rail were missing and casts were made and the joints held together provisionally with iron collars which Bell hoped to remove once the whole quadrangle was protected from encroachment by wandering cattle by erection of a wire fence. In the second season the work was completed by reassembling and erecting the eight curving columns which represented lotus stalks and which terminated in half-opened buds which originally supported the wooden roof. On the completion of the work, Bell's satisfaction is evident from his report: 'After the most tedious sorting and resorting, of the countless fragments lying *perdu* far around, the scattered pieces of the coping of the basement, and many broken sections and lesser portions of the beautiful lotus-columns, were recovered: these *disjecta membra* were then fitted together and the shrine restored almost as it stood of old, save for its roof'.

Restorations were also carried out in the 'Citadel' area which lies between the Promontory and the Quadrangle. Here stood the 'Raja-Maligawa'. Bell wrote that 'with its bold *makara* wings and lion-guarded staircase it is among Buddhistic stone ruins of Polonnaruwa second only in elegance and profusion of sculpture to the unique Watadage'. The two great dagabas, Kiri Vihara and Rankot Vihara were cleared of vegetation in 1905. Further work on Kiri Vihara was undertaken in 1910 (Figure 15).

Fig 15 - Jetawanarama and Kiri Dagabas during restoration

Scaffolding was set up around the bell and the many wide fissures cleaned out in preparation for re-filling. Bell was unable to complete the repairs but all danger from water penetrating the Dagaba was prevented by essential work carried out in 1911-12.

The site at Polonnaruwa which moved Bell most was the Gal Vihara which he started excavating in 1907. He described the site as follows in a report to the RASCB: 'The colossal figures and rock-hewn shrine of this picturesquely wooded site renders it probably the most impressive antiquity preserved in Ceylon. Altogether four images exist carved from the live rock. Two are *ot-pilima or* sedent figures of the Buddha. The largest, 15ft. 3in. by 14ft. 8in., is seated cross-legged meditative *mudra*, upon an elaborate *asanaya*, beneath an elaborately carved *torana* (arch) of *makara* design; the other, in similar attitude, is at the back of a rock-hewn shrine. The third on the extreme right is a recumbent image, 46 ft. 2in.from head to toe. The figure is represented in orthodox fashion, lying on its right side, with right arm and hand on a pillow under the head, the left arm being straightened along the body.

But it is the solitary life-like figure, traditionally styled Ananda, the favourite disciple of the Buddha, standing erect with crossed arm on a lotus pedestal 24 ft. from the rock floor, which appeals specially to the imagination, from its sorrow-stricken expression and natural attitude of deep mourning. This statue is, *par excellence*, the most artistic and well conceived to be found anywhere in the islands'.

In his annual report for 1907 he goes even further in his praise of this group of stone figures and declared them: 'possibly not rivalled throughout the continent of India'. He wrote thus: 'The line of gigantic figures carved from the grey rock which forms their background, calm, immovable, majestic, amid the hush of the surrounding forest, gazing ever fixedly into space with the pensiveness of profound meditation, or wrapped in eternal slumber, must inspire the thoughtful beholder wonder and admiration, mingled with an instinctive sense of silent awe'.

Bell's Annual reports were very detailed and thorough. He described what the excavations entailed and how they were undertaken. What was found was described in great detail. He noted the findings of earlier explorers. The significance of what was found was considered by comparing the findings with historical texts, particularly the *Mahawansa*. He recorded what restorations were undertaken. The reports also contained epigraphic evidence and translations. The 1905 Report consisted of 79 pages of text, 36 photographic plates and a map. However, his reports were frequently late; the 1905 report was not published till 1909. He was often criticised by the Governor for the lateness of his reports. The delays were partly due to a lack of assistance in early years and partly due to his repeated ill health. It was also probably the case that he preferred supervising field work to writing them up.

The search for Bell's successor started as early as 1908. The obvious candidate, John Still, had resigned from the Department and was no longer available. The Governor, H E McCallum, asked Sir John Marshall if he could recommend anyone from his own staff but Marshall replied that he could not spare anyone. Bell, himself, was keen that he should be succeeded by H W Codrington, a Civil Servant, who was an expert on numismatics and had an extensive knowledge of Kandyan history. The Colonial Office was determined that Bell's successor should be a professional archaeologist. After several names were considered, the choice fell on E R A Ayrton, who had spent seven years excavating in Egypt. Bell's retirement was postponed for a year to allow Ayrton to study Pali, Sanskrit, Sinhalese and Tamil as well as Indian and Ceylonese Epigraphy. In the event he spent two years at Oxford and in Germany and with the Archaeological Survey of India and joined the Archaeological Survey of Ceylon in March 1912. He took over from Bell in December 1912. Tragically, given all the training he had received, he drowned while out shooting near Tissamaharama tank in May 1914.

The British Government was too occupied with the Great War to find a successor hence in the interregnum till 1921, when A M Hocart was appointed, D A L Perera was left in charge under the nominal supervision of the Government Agent for the North-Central Province. Though it may seem surprising a local person was trusted with the running of the Department, in the case of Perera, he had been effectively Bell's deputy and had stood in for him during his bouts of illness. Bell, himself, had the highest opinion of his local staff as demonstrated in a testimonial he wrote about them in 1917: 'The Ceylon Government has been very fortunate in the three draughtsmen attached to the Archaeological Survey, to whose joint efforts – each in his degree and line – demanding much patience, perseverance, and a talent beyond the ordinary. The Island is indebted for the possession of a perfect series, in worthy reproduction, of these unique paintings of a bygone day – now, alas, fast disappearing – which in beauty of execution, in wealth of colour, and skilful technique, originally approached – though possibly they did not quite rival – the magnificent Indian frescoes at Ajanta.

In their mutual and highly successful collaboration, Messrs. D A Perera, W M Fernando and P G Perera have done real honour no less to themselves than to the Archaeological Survey Department and to the Government which they served so well. To all interested in Ceylon of a past day, who care to visit the Colombo Museum, full and easy opportunity is at length afforded of studying closely the finest examples of ancient and mediaeval painting still surviving in the Island'.

Following his retirement he continued to live in Sri Lanka and spent the first few years completing his Annual Reports. He lived mainly in Kandy but spent some time in Anuradhapura. The Report for 1911-12 was published in 1915. He continued as Honorary Secretary of the Journal of the RASCB till 1914. He served on the Management Committee of the Colombo Museum till 1922. From 1915 till 1916 he was co-editor with John M Senaveratne of a new journal *Ceylon Antiquary and Literary Register*. He continued involvement of the repairs to the Jetawanarama at Polonnaruwa. Throughout his career he had a passion for the Maldive Islands and visited them several times. He published a series of articles in the Journal of the RASCB with the running title *Excerpta Maldiviana*. Bell spent his final years, until he died aged eighty four in 1937, producing his monumental work *The Maldive Islands: Monograph on the History, Archaeology and Epigraphy*. The book was not, in fact, published until 1940, three years after his death, having been completed by his clerk W L de Silva.

Many tributes were paid to him in the press in formal obituaries but one of the most moving was published in a local paper at the time of his retirement: 'Apart from the light he has thrown upon the history of this Island, he has restored much that was forgotten in its religion, for he has laid the land under a lasting debt of gratitude by his sympathetic interest and his careful preservation of the relics of the ancient times. What he has recovered from the destructive grasp of time is not merely of historical interest: much of it is rated higher than history, for it is sacred and holy, and the object of reverence to a living religion. Here, good fortune favoured him, for it is seldom that an archaeologist dives into the dead past to retrieve what belongs to a living faith. The treasures of Egypt are concerned with a dead cult; of Greece with a discredited mythology; of Mexico and Yucatan with discarded heathen worship. But the religion which erected the monuments recovered by Mr Bell is living and a power still. That placed him in a situation of unexampled delicacy, and called for qualities of tact, forbearance and patience such as no worker in the same field has ever had to exhibit. It is his distinction that, on the whole, he has emerged creditably from the unusual test'.

## Archaeological Survey of Ceylon – post Bell

As soon as he assumed his duties, Ayrton began the conservation on Ratnaprasada, hitherto known as Elephant Stables. Firstly, he had to reset the disturbed stone slabs which formed the facing of the platform. The guardstone and the moonstone of the north flight of steps were laid in and reset on the beds of concrete. This was followed by excavations at the western Monasteries. Here he excavated fourteen buildings and the excavations yielded an inscription of one line containing five letters. Paleographically he ascribed them to the $10^{th}$ century AD. He commented on the importance of the dating: 'In Anuradhapura the number of buildings to which dates can be assigned, even approximately, is so small, that it is very satisfactory that we are even able to suggest possible dates for all the buildings excavated during the past fifteen months'. The Samadhi Buddha was want only broken into pieces by treasure seekers in September 1913. It was restored though some fragments were so crushed that their place had to taken with cement, the head luckily being unspoilt.

Following the death of Ayrton, major excavations and conservation did not commence till the appointment of A M Hocart as Archaeological Commissioner in 1922. Further work on the Thuparama Vihara at Anuradhapura was sanctioned by the Governor and commenced in 1922 to 23. This involved pointing works, positioning of columns and resetting the entrance. The Nakha Vihara which had been excavated earlier was now conserved. Hocart also started conservation work at the Jetavanarama Vihara. He generally followed methods adopted by Bell. The work included restoration of the damaged parts of the south wall, consolidation of the foundation of the south-west wall and restoration of the large cracks that had developed on the western wall. Work was needed in the interior of the shrine and the walls of the corridor. Some parts of the robe of the Buddha image needed consolidation. In the next year the conservation of the Kaludiya Pokuna cave was completed. The Samadhi Buddha statue which was in a state of deterioration was made waterproof. At Polonnaruwa some damaged parts of the King's Palace and important sections of the Citadel were repaired.

Hocart left the Department in 1924 and he was replaced by E R Sudbury. He started the conservation of the Hatadage at Polonnaruwa. By this time, a number of stone slabs had fallen down. Sudbury observed that it was not easy to pick them out and find their proper place by measurement. The only certain way was actually fitting the stones together and this could only be done during the course of the rebuilding. A number of difficulties were encountered. Most of the original details of the building had been destroyed obliterating the original information. There was a shortage of skilled masons and inadequate number of labourers. Sudbury also worked on the Western Monasteries at Anurdhapura. Missing stones of the retaining walls of the pond had to be replaced concrete faced with cement and gravel.

Hocart returned in 1925. He worked on the dome of the Thuparama at Polonnaruwa which was treated with a patent water-proofing composition for the brick work. After two years the process had to be repeated. Work was required on the stone ramp of the Quadrangle at Polonnaruwa. The south-west portion of this rampart had been conserved by Ayrton. More work had to be done by Hocart. He supervised the ongoing work at the Hatadage. Extensive pointing work was required on the terraced wall of the Buddhasma Pasada. Some damaged parts of the King's Palace and important sections of the Citadel were repaired by Hocart. In addition to work at the archaeological sites, a Research and Publications section of the Department was established. Coming within its scope were the exploration of archaeological monuments, identification of artefacts, dating and further studies, the maintenance of a library, developing a catalogue of photographs and negatives of monuments, an archive to stock personal files, diaries etc. of the staff, the maintenance of Archaeological Museums and, the most important of all, the production of publications.

The Department of Archaeology in the 1930s was dominated by A H Longhurst and Dr S Paranavitana. The latter was the first Sri Lankan to be appointed to the post and he went on to be in charge of the Department till 1956. Even under others, Paranivatana's contribution to the work of the Department was considerable. The majority of the British Archaeological Commissioners who preceded him were scholars and indefatigable workers, zealously devoted to archaeology. Sri Lanka was fortunate that the first Sri Lankan Head was not second to them in erudition, enthusiasm or dedication.

The annual expenditure of the Department reflected to some extent the global economic climate of the times. In the financial year 1929-30 a sum of just over one hundred thousand rupees was spent but in the following years this amount was not reached. This was due to the global depression but as the global economy recovered for the five years following 1935-36, expenditure reached the hundred thousand rupees. At the commencement of the War, expenditure slumped for 1940-41 and 1941-42. However, stationing of foreign troops and running of various military establishments brought in money for the Island and from 1942-43 onwards, the hundred thousand rupee sum was exceeded. In the financial year 1946-47 the country was so prosperous that it was possible to expand the activities of the Department and expenditure exceeded five hundred thousand rupees.

The work undertaken at Anuradhapura in the 1930s included clearing the street between the Thuparama Dagaba and Ruwanveliseya. The conservation of the remains of the image-house to the west of the Jetavanaramaya was completed in 1930. Trial excavations were conducted at the site of the Samadi Statue. The broken pedestal of the statue was rebuilt and the statue re-set in 1930. The statue was chemically treated in 1935. Another large mutilated sedent Buddha statue was found in the jungle west of the Abhayagiri Dagaba fallen from its pedestal. A new pedestal was built with the old bricks found at the site and the statue placed on it. The jungle around the statue was cleared in 1936. The statues were encircled with iron railings. The Buddhist railing site near the Jetavanara Dagaba was cleared and the remains were conserved in 1937. The entire group of buildings in the monastic site miscalled Queen's Palace was conserved in 1938. The best preserved and most tastefully executed moonstone was discovered so far was at this site. The sculpture of this moonstone was reproduced on the five rupee coin minted in 1957 to commemorate the Buddha Jayanthi.

At Polonnaruwa excavations were undertaken from 1932 in an extensive area of structures forming part of the palace complex of Parakramabahu I. The building in the north-eastern part of the quadrangle was identified for the first time as the Rajaveshyaphujanga Mandapaya from an inscription found on it. The evidence here showed that the original structure put up by Parakramabahu I was reconstructed some distance away from its original position by Parakramabahu II. The eastern entrance of the quadrangle was excavated, conserved and kept open for public use. Longhurst removed the debris which had blocked the entrance to the Tivanka Pilgrimage and conserved it. He also excavated and conserved the Pabalu Vihara. Among the finds here was a gilt bronze miniature stupa which Longhurst presumed to be the model of the Pabalu Vihara. He also did extensive repairs on the Kiri Vihara. Some further excavations were done at the Rankot Vihara where the Vahalkadas and the shrine of the recumbent Buddha statue were conserved. Longhurst replastered the walls at the Thuparama, Lankatilaka and the Tivalanka Pilgrimage. The roads were widened and an effort made to plant shade trees on either side of the roads. A new road was laid from the King's Palace to Lankatilaka following the ancient road to some extent.

Sigiriya had begun to attract foreign tourists and local visitors by the third decade. Yet, this once great Capital of Sri Lanka was limited to a few sleepy villages nestling among jungles. Wild elephants roamed the jungle dealing death to a villager or two, once in a while. The work of copying and studying graffiti on the gallery walls at Sigiriya, already in hand, was continued. By 1930 about a hundred verses from the eighth and ninth centuries had been deciphered and much progress made in interpreting them. In 1931 an iron ladder was fixed to the fresco pocket, with a protective cover of expanded metal. In 1938 this ladder was replaced with a spiral staircase. In 1936 the large pond on the summit was cleared and made to hold water once more. The remains of the Palace of Kassapa are the earliest secular remains in Sri Lanka. Bell excavated these remains from 1895-7 but under the very trying conditions, at the time, did not conserve them. These remains were conserved in 1947.

The Department made the sites as attractive and accessible as possible. Wherever the jungle was cleared, the Commissioners took pains to leave shady trees at convenient intervals. Longhurst cleared the jungle around the Mahanaga Pabbata Vihara at Sigiriya and the monastic site beyond it and made a mile long footpath connecting them which he said 'makes a delightful walk through the beautiful forest'. Speaking of the Demala Maha Seya at Polonnaruwa, he wrote 'the view from the top of the mound is superb and the site is worth clearing of jungle if only for this reason, as there are no hills at Polonnaruwa and therefore no extensive views'. In Paranavitana's time, particularly, it was felt that the sites should be made to look attractive and provided with motorable roads to facilitate site-seeing. Efforts were made to plant ornamental and flowering plants with Paranavitana selecting trees referred in ancient literature as growing on the sites.

One index by which the public judges the work of the Department is by the standard of publications. The scholarly publications of the Department were very high during the 30s and 40s. They were produced regularly except during the war years. They included *Temple of the Tooth, Kandy* by Hocart (1931), *Excavations in the Citadel of Anuradhapura* by Paranavitana (1936) *The Stupa in Ceylon* by Paranavitana (1946). A popular book entitled *The Story of the Stupa* was published by Longhurst (1936) but this was not a departmental publication.

## Colombo Museum

In addition to the restoration of the ancient cities, a further important contribution of the British was the founding of the Colombo Museum by Governor Gregory in 1877. Gregory's education was steeped in the Classics. This background resulted in him having an admiration for ancient literature, sculpture, and past cultures and kindled in him an abiding interest in antiquities and the learning of the past ages. Soon after his arrival, he showed a keen interest in Kandyan architecture. He had the walls around the Government Agent's residence in Kandy and other walls, especially along the lake, which had originally been constructed in the Kandyan style but were now in a state of disrepair, restored.

In Sri Lanka he found ideal conditions for establishing a museum as the economy was flourishing. He initiated the project in the first year of his administration and presented a compelling case to the Legislative Council. Everybody recognised the need for an establishment for housing exhibits representing Sri Lanka's natural history, antiquities and industries. The Council approved and Gregory embarked on the scheme. He had not obtained prior approval from the Colonial Office, which was concerned that, as the colony was already embarking on expensive ventures such as the breakwater in Colombo and the extension of the railways, the cost of the museum might strain the island's exchequer. The project was halted and further clarification sought. Gregory was determined to complete the project. He sought to convince the Colonial Office. He emphasised that the institution was indispensible for housing material for scientific and antiquarian research. It would safely house the Ceylon Branch of the Royal Asiatic Society's collections, the Oriental Library and other useful books. It would also furnish space to conduct academic meetings, exhibitions and lectures. Donations would provide exhibits and it would entail only modest expenditure and would not jeopardise essential public works. Rumours began to circulate that the Colonial Office was opposing the venture and adverse press reports began to be published. Although lamenting the expenditure needed, The Secretary of State sanctioned the project.

Fig 16 - Colombo Museum

The design of the building was entrusted to the Government Architect, Mr Smither, but throughout the Governor exercised personal supervision. The museum was completed in 1875 (Figure 16). It was a singularly beautiful and bright building, well ventilated with adequate provision for lighting. To furnish exhibits, ancient sculptures and artefacts from Anuradhapura and Polonnaruwa were collected. Many of these objects were in danger of being destroyed during road construction schemes or of being looted by treasure seekers. Gregory's action proved most opportune in saving valuable examples of ancient art and sculpture. In the first year alone, ninety nine thousand people visited the institution.

Encouraged by European and English scholars who were interested in studying Sri Lanka's languages and culture, Gregory ardently fostered the cause of research. He ordered epigraphs to be copied and supported archaeological excavation and restoration. Ancient historical chronicles were copied, edited and translated; books and manuscripts sought and preserved. The photographs of the Buddhist remains at Anuradhapura and Polonnaruwa which had been taken during Robinson's governorship were compiled into two volumes with a commentary. In 1873, Anuradhapura was surveyed and objects of interest were indicated on a map. Detailed plans and sections of dagabas were made. Lithographical copies were sent to the British Museum for the reference of scholars.

The founding of the museum enabled local people and visitors to appreciate in detail the culture and heritage of Sri Lanka. Furthermore, for the first time in the modern age, books were published describing the ancient cities. In Sir James Emerson Tennent's *Ceylon* (1859), Part X, which contains 62 pages, is devoted to the ruined cities. There are beautiful engravings of all the sites. The first book specifically written describing the historical sites was *The Buried Cities of Ceylon* by S M Burrows which was published in 1885. It contains a detailed description of the sites, essential visitor information and places everything in historical context by frequent references to the *Mahavansa*. This publication was followed by *Ruined Cities of Ceylon* (1897) by H Cave, *Ancient Capitals of Ceylon* (1907) by John Still and *Ancient Ceylon* (1909) by H Parker. The sale of these books in Britain and elsewhere meant that people throughout the world could learn about and appreciate the magnificence of Sri Lanka's past.

The rediscovery and the restoration of Sri Lanka's historic sites were outstanding achievements by the British. It is not surprising that Pandit Nandadeva Wijesekera, who was Editor-in-Chief of the Commemorative Series for the Centenary of the Archaeological Department paid the following eloquent tribute to the colonial authorities: 'For the first time in centuries, people were able to appreciate the unique paintings on the Rock at Sigiriya, the stone images of the Buddha at Anuradhapura, stupendous dagabas at Anuradhapura, Polonnaruwa and the beautiful rock carvings.

All these objects of both antiquarian and artistic beauty, historical importance and cultural value revealed in unmistakable terms evidence of the glorious past of the Sinhalese. The colonial authorities admired all that they discovered and the people of the Island were reawakened to behold, admire and wonder at the sight of the creative genius of their forefathers.

No one should fail to remember with gratitude the services rendered by the colonial powers who were responsible for overseeing the protection and preservation of ancient monuments. The credit for this far sighted policy and close attention must be given to the highest administrators of the island during the beginning of the Department. These, of course, include the Governor himself. This enlightened policy and responsible attitude have been responsible in great measure for the protection and preservation of the ancient monuments at Anuradhapura, Sigiriya and Polonnaruwa. It is indeed a policy well worth continuing and even emulation by the present Government'.

## Study of Sacred Texts

At the time of their arrival, the British were totally unaware of the abundance of Pali chronicles to be found in Sri Lanka. The situation changed when Sir James Emerson Tennent wrote his masterly work on Ceylon in 1826 and news was communicated to Europe that 'whilst the history of India was only to be conjectured from myths and elaborated from dates on copper grants, or fading inscriptions on rocks and columns, Ceylon was in possession of continuous written chronicles, rich in authentic facts and not only assigning a connected history of the island itself, but also yielding valuable materials for elucidation that of India'. The credit for this epiphany must be given to George Turnour who at the time made public his discovery of the *Mahavansa*.

Turnour was born in Sri Lanka in 1799. He was sent to England for his education, returned in 1820 and joined the Civil Service. After a succession of posts he became Government Agent for the Central Province and was stationed in Kandy in 1833. He came across the *Mahavansa* while he was stationed in Ratnapura from 1825-27. At the opening of the 19th century, the existence of the *Mahavansa* or *Great Dynasty* was only known to a handful of Buddhist monks and none had translated it. It was a metrical chronicle, hiding in mystical verse, the most astonishing dynastic history of any people, covering a period of twenty-three centuries from the year 543 BC to 1758 AD. One learned priest recognised the genius of the Civil Servant and told him that a 'tika' – a prose explanation was still in existence and if it could be found, it might be possible to understand the chronicle. Turnour's interest was aroused and the two of them searched for the document which was discovered in a vihara at Mulgirigalla. Even with the 'tika' the task he faced was considerable. Though Turnour was fluent in both spoken and written Sinhalese, he knew nothing of Pali. There were no text books, dictionaries or parallel documents to study. There were only a few Buddhists priests who knew Pali and with their help he embarked on the task. He first published a paper entitled *An Epitome of the History of Ceylon* in 1833 and for the first time this contained the chronology of the long line of Sinhala rulers. He went on to translate the first third of the chronicle, which was published in 1837. This was the first authentic translation of the *Mahavansa* and was crucial in enabling James Prinsep in India to identify the Emperor Asoka (*vide supra*).

There had been an earlier translation of the *Mahavansa* in Edward Upham's three volume work *The Sacred and Historical Books of Ceylon*. But it was full of inaccuracies. The Introduction of Turnour's *Mahavansa* contained a short dissertation on the Pali language. In the Appendix he gave a detailed account of the *Tipitaka*. Most of all, he drew the attention of scholars that there was no part of the world which had greater facilities to study Pali than in Sri Lanka. In addition to the historical importance of the language, which had hitherto been little understood, there existed many doctrinal works on Buddhism still being extensively and critically studied by the Buddhist clergy.

Surprisingly, other early British residents in Sri Lanka who took an interest in Buddhism, Sinhalese and Pali were the Christian missionaries. Their number included Charter, Lambick, Clough, Spence Hardy and Gogerly. Early publications included Charter's *Sinhalese Grammar* (1815); Clough's *Pali Grammar* (1824) and *Sinhalese Dictionary* (1821); Lambick's *Sinhalese Grammar* (1834); Hardy's *Manual of Buddhism* (1860); Copleston's *Theravada Buddhism* (1892) and Gogerly's *Ceylon Buddhism* (1908). Though they studied Sinhalese, Pali and wrote about Buddhism to challenge and supplant the religion, when these books reached Europe and America, they aroused in the hearts of scholars there a desire to learn more about the religion that the missionaries sought to condemn and the literature of which these books formed a part. The missionaries, themselves, eventually began to respect the rationality of Buddhism.

As in India, the British clergymen and civil servants, who for the most part had been educated in the Classics, were fascinated by the richness of Sri Lankan and Buddhist culture. As was common in Britain, they decided to form a learned society, The Ceylon Branch of the Royal Asiatic Society, to discuss their findings and publish papers. This initiated the first systematic and academic study of Sri Lankan culture and heritage. The credit for the formation of the Society must be given to W. Knighton, who in the same year had published a History of Ceylon and was the first Secretary and John Capper who became the first Treasurer. Other early enthusiastic supporters were the clergymen, Spence Hardy and Gogerly. The aims of the society were 'to institute and promote enquiries into the History, Religions, Languages, Literature, Arts, Sciences and Social Conditions of the present and former inhabitants of the Island of Ceylon'. In the first meeting, two papers were read, by Rev. W Gogerly and Mr Knighton on Buddhism and Ceylon literature respectively.

The Society began with thirty-four members, all European. At its inception it may have seemed slightly patronising affair for Europeans to study 'the natives of Ceylon, their manners and customs' but it rapidly became a very different entity. Its members soon included learned Ceylonese, such as James D'Alwis and Simon Cassie Chitty, who had compiled the *Ceylon Gazetteer*. Later members included men of distinction such as H M Fernando, C M Fernando and W A de Silva. The Society's Patron was the Governor and its President, eminent men such as Sir Ponnambalam Arunachalam. Early papers included ones by Spence Hardy on Sinhalese language and literature, Gogerly on Buddhism, founded on his study of Pali; Brodie read out his results of his finds of rock inscriptions; James D'Alwis and Cassie Chitty had each read about ten papers on different subjects, displaying the breadth of their scholarship; while on the scientific side, E L Layard and E F Kelaart reported on their studies on natural history. Capper, himself, seems to have had a variety of interests and read papers on subjects as far apart as ravages of the coconut beetle and the revenue system of the Dutch. In the last decades of the 19th century, members included Hugh Nevill, W Ferguson, Lieut. Legge, Louis de Zoysa, L F Lee and Rhys Davids. In the early decades of the twentieth century increasing number of papers began to be read by prominent Sri

Lankans such as W A de Silva and Paul Pieris. The former was interested in many aspects of Sinhalese language and culture and the latter on the Portuguese period. Perhaps the most outstanding member of the Society was H C P Bell who served as Secretary and contributed his first paper in 1883 and his last one in 1935.

The meetings of the Society, which were generally held at the Colombo Museum, afforded both Europeans and Sri Lankans the opportunity to share their fascination for the country's culture and heritage. They were frequently attended by the Governor and high British officials. The discussions following the presentation of the talks demonstrate that senior British officials were deeply interested in and knowledgeable on the subjects under consideration.

Though Sri Lanka contained a wealth of Pali texts, they were scattered in pansalas and pirivenas throughout the island. There was no central catalogue listing the texts and specifying where they were stored. The first attempt to prepare a catalogue of Sri Lanka's literary works was made by Rev. Spence Hardy, who in the course of his 20 year stay on the island, made a note of whatever manuscripts he happened to come across. At a meeting of the Ceylon Branch of the Royal Asiatic Society in February 1848, he read out a list compiled by him of *Books in the Pali and Sinhalese Languages*. This list was published in the Journal the same year. In 1852, James D'Alwis, one of the most erudite scholars of the age, published his monumental work, an English translation of Vedaha's Sinhalese grammar, the *Sidat-sangara*. In the Introduction, which extended for over two hundred pages, he gave a continuous history of Sinhala books from the earliest time to his own day. Unfortunately, he confined himself to Sinhalese works and did not include Pali texts.

In 1868, during the governorship of Sir Hercules Robinson, Louis de Zoysa, Maha Mudaliyar and Chief Translator to the Government of Ceylon was asked for the necessity of the inspection of library shelves of pansalas in Ceylon. He reported in 1869 that: 'If some scheme as that adopted by the Indian Government be applied not only to the Sanskrit but also to Pali and Sinhalese manuscripts of the country, there is every reason to believe that many important historical and other works which are not now accessible to the learned may be brought to light'. Robinson recognised the need for a 'Descriptive Catalogue of the Pali, Sinhalese and Sanskrit

Manuscripts' to be found in the libraries of the pansalas and other places in Sri Lanka. He made such a proposal to the Colonial Office in London and suggested that James D'Alwis should undertake the task (Figure 17). The Secretary of State for the Colonies, The Earl Granville, agreed. It is interesting to note that Granville's reply assenting to the proposal included a copy of *Buddhaghosa's Parables* by Max Muller which he thought might be of interest to Robinson. Clearly, British officials at the highest levels were aware of important Buddhist texts.

CEYLON.

CORRESPONDENCE

BETWEEN

THE GOVERNOR OF CEYLON

AND

THE SECRETARY OF STATE FOR THE COLONIES,

WITH REFERENCE TO THE PREPARATION OF A

DESCRIPTIVE CATALOGUE OF THE PÁLI, SINHALESE, AND SANSKRIT MANUSCRIPTS,

TO BE FOUND IN THE LIBRARIES OF THE PANSALAS (BUDDHIST MONASTERIES), AND OTHER PLACES IN CEYLON.

Presented to both Houses of Parliament by Command of Her Majesty,
*July* 4, 1870.

LONDON:
PRINTED BY WILLIAM CLOWES & SONS, STAMFORD STREET AND CHARING CROSS,
FOR HER MAJESTY'S STATIONERY OFFICE.
1870.

Fig 17 - UK Parliamentary Paper relating to the Catalogue of Pali Manuscripts

D'Alwis published the first volume of a *Descriptive Catalogue of Sanskrit, Pali and Sinhalese Literary Works of Ceylon* in 1870. He had written descriptive accounts of twenty-three books including the *Mahavansa* and *Dipavansa*. Unfortunately, he died before he could complete the task. D'Alwis also recommended to the Government the desirability of forming a Library of Pali, Sanskrit and Sinhalese works. Robinson agreed to the proposal and in 1870 the Legislative Council voted funds for immediate expenditure for the establishment of the Government Oriental Library. Mr Louis de Zoyza was appointed Librarian. A sum of over Rs 30,000 was spent purchasing manuscripts and getting copies made of manuscripts. A number were also donated to the Library.

Shortly before, in 1868, some of the most learned Bhikkhus and laymen, including Ven. Hikkaduwa Sri Sumangala, Ven. Weligama Sri Sumangala and Ven. Vaskaduve Subhuti Thera assembled in Palmadulla and made a revision of Buddhist texts. Within a year they completed the revision of the books on Vinaya Pitaka, both the Texts and Commentaries.

In 1873, the Government directed Louis de Zoysa, the Librarian of the Government Oriental Library, to inspect temple libraries and find particulars of literary treasures they contained. He visited a large number of temple libraries throughout the island. On the whole he was met favourably by the heads of the monasteries but in some he was received with distrust, the monks evidently suspecting that the Government had designs upon their collections. He, too, died before the task was completed but the Government issued as much of the catalogue as had been completed in 1876. Mr M de Z Wickremasinghe, then Assistant Librarian of the Colombo Museum Library was asked to complete the work started by de Zoysa. He visited the temples that de Zoysa had been unable to visit. The final compilation was embodied in the Administration Reports of the Colombo Museum 1890-95.

As a result of these endeavours valuable manuscripts containing useful information on Buddhism and Sri Lanka's past were procured or copied and preserved in the Museum. The Sinhalese, Pali and Sanskrit works gathered in the Museum were catalogued. Copies of the list were circulated to the British Museum and other Western libraries so that foreign scholars would learn about the valuable literature in Sri Lanka. Governor Gregory arranged for the Mahavansa to be translated into Sinhala. This was published in two volumes in 1883. In order to understand the text, a study of its commentary, the 'tika', was essential. Gregory entrusted a revision of the commentary to Ven. Hikkaduwa Sumangala and Pandit Batuwantudawa.

Gregory's endeavours kindled local interest in pursuing Oriental studies. Monks and Chiefs collected donations and established a Pali library in Kandy. The Governor assisted this enterprise by providing a room for storing the books and for the use of scholars. In Colombo, an Oriental College was founded in 1877. Attended by monks and laymen, for which an annual grant of Rs 600 was authorised by the Governor, this institution grew into rich centre of Oriental learning. Today, it has blossomed into the Vidyodaya University. Governor Gordon was equally enthusiastic to translate oriental texts. He arranged for Mudaliyar Wijesinha to translate the remainder of the *Mahavansa* which Turnour had not translated into English. The translation was published in 1889 and dedicated to Gordon. John Still published an Index to this translation in 1907. In 1902 S M Burrows, Director of Public Instruction, established the Committee on Oriental Studies to systemise the instruction given at various Pirivenas.

The British enthusiasm for translating ancient texts encouraged the Sinhalese Buddhists to publish their own books with Sinhalese characters. The first Sinhala press was the Lankapora Press, established in Galle in 1862 with funding from the King of Burma. About the same time the Sarwagna Sasanabhiwurdhi Dayaka press was established in Kotahena by Ven. Migettuwatte Unnanse. The Lakrivikirana Press was established in 1863 and later the Lankabhinna Press. The first Pali work of importance to be published was the Abhidhanappadipika by Ven. Subhuti Nayaka Unnanse in 1865. The Pirit Pota (a collection of suttas), which is very popular among Buddhists, was published by Lankabhinna Press in 1865. In the early years the Sinhalese Press published some Pali texts and two classes of works with a certain degree of abundance, namely Grammars and individual suttas with descriptive and detailed translations.

## Pali Scholars

Several British Officials became renowned Pali scholars. Their efforts greatly contributed to the understanding of Buddhist texts by scholars in Sri Lanka and elsewhere. R C Childers became well known after he published in 1872 and 1875 his two-volume Dictionary of the Pali language. The work was dedicated to Edward VII, then Price of Wales, who had visited Sri Lanka at the time. It contained Prefaces in English and Sinhalese, the latter containing a valuable historical account of works on Pali grammar either written in Ceylon itself or used there. It was indispensible for the study Pali and Buddhist texts. It remained a primary source of reference for the next forty years. Childers entered the Ceylon Civil Service in 1856. In his spare time he studied Pali and was impressed by the beauty and sublime quality of the Buddha's teaching enshrined in the Pali cannon. He resigned in 1864 and returned to England where he engaged himself in Pali scholarship. He became a Professor at University College, London. One of his earlier works was a translation of the *Khuddaka Patha* which was published in the Journal of the Royal Asiatic Society in 1870.

The foremost of the British Pali Scholars was T W Rhys Davids. He was born in England and went to Germany as a student to study Sanskrit and obtained a Ph.D. He entered the Ceylon Civil Service in 1864. A curious incident while he serving as a District Judge led him to study Pali. A case in connection with a village Buddhist temple came before him involving ecclesiastical law and a document in a language which no one present could read was presented in evidence. Rhys Davids decided to learn Pali and the monk who taught him was Ven. Yatramulle Unnanse who lived in Bentota who had earlier taught Pali to Childers. The monk was gravely ill but Childers had told Davids that his learning was 'perfectly astonishing'. Moreover, to both Childers and Davids, Ven. Unnanse epitomised the very essence of the Buddhist ideal of mendicancy. The monk rarely left his temple and avoided publicity. His personality also left an indelible impression on Rhys Davids. In a lecture in England much later Davids said: 'When he first came to see me, the hand of death was already upon him. He was sinking into the grave from the effects of a painful and incurable malady. I had heard of his learning as a Pali scholar, and of his illness, and was grateful for him for leaving his home, under such circumstances, to teach a stranger. There was a strange light in his sunken eyes, and he was constantly turning away from questions of Pali to questions of Buddhism. I found him versed in all the poetry and ethics of the Suttas, and was glad to hear him talk. There was an indescribable attraction, a high-mindedness that filled me with reverence'.

He resigned from the Ceylon Civil Service in 1872, returned to England, studied law and was called to The Bar in 1877. His practice was poor and he concentrated on his Buddhist studies. He contributed to the Journal of the Royal Asiatic Society with papers on *Inscriptions of Parakrama Bahu, Sigiri, the Lion Rock* and *Two Old Sinhalese Inscriptions* which brought him recognition as a knowledgeable scholar. He surveyed the labours in Pali and Sinhalese of earlier scholars such as Turnour, Gogerly, Spence Hardy and Childers.

Rhys Davids read widely on the history of Buddhism and gained a greater mastery of Pali. This he did despite attacks of malaria which he had contracted in Sri Lanka. The first book he wrote was *The Ancient Coins and Measures of Ceylon* which appeared in 1877 and then his *Manual of Buddhism* the following year. By now he had gained a high reputation and was corresponding with an increasing circle of Pali scholars. He translated the *Jataka Nidanakatha* with an important introduction on the history of Birth-story literature. Next year he contributed a translation of Buddhist Suttas from the Pali to the Sacred Books of the Buddhist Series edited by Max Muller. Between 1881 and 1885 he published in the same series three volumes entitled *Vinaya Texts* which he translated in collaboration with Hermann Oldenberg.

He delivered six lectures under The Hibbert Trust in 1881 and emphasized some of what he had gained and written about in his *Manual of Buddhism* three years earlier. In the second lecture he announced the formation of the Pali Text Society. Eminent scholars from both the West and the East welcomed the society. Offers of financial assistance came from various sources and Pali scholars of many nationalities offered their free services to edit and translate the texts. Rhys Davids described the importance of the texts as follows: 'The historical importance of these texts can scarcely be exaggerated, either in respect of their value for the history of folk-lore, or of religion, or of language. It is already certain that they were all put into their present form within a very limited period extending to less than a century and a half (about 400-250 BC). For that period they have preserved for us, quite uncontaminated by any outside influence, of everyday beliefs and customs of a people nearly related to ourselves just as they were passing through the first stages of civilization. They are our best authorities for the early history of that interesting system of religion so nearly allied to some of our latest speculations among ourselves, and which has influenced so powerfully and for so long a time so great a portion of the human race – the system of religion we now call Buddhism'.

Rhys Davids helped the Pali Text Society publish almost the whole of the Pali Canon and a considerable number of commentaries and English translations. He, himself, edited and translated numerous texts. He served the Society with devotion for forty-one years. The *Pali-English Dictionary* which the Society brought out stands as a monument to him. He began to compile it at the age of seventy-two and lived to see the publication of the first three parts of this magnificent work. It was completed three years after his death by his friend William Stede.

Rhys Davids became the first President of the Buddhist Society of Great Britain and Ireland which was founded in 1907. The aims of the Society were to extend knowledge of the tenets of Buddhism and the promotion of the study of the Pali language. The Society held meetings and produced a quarterly journal *The Buddhist Review*. The Society had very illustrious high officials. Its Patron was the King of Siam and the Vice-Presidents included the Prince of Sikkim and the Earl of Mexborough. By the 1920s, Sri Lankans occupied senior positions. W A de Silva was the President and D B Jayatilaka was a Vice–President.

Rhys Davids married his wife Caroline in 1894. She was not only his companion for a quarter of a century but was also as proficient in the field of Pali scholarship as he was. A woman of remarkable intellect and tireless energy, she edited and translated some of the most abstruse texts, besides writing several thought-provoking original books. He, with the collaboration of his wife, completed a translation of the *Digha Nikaya* called *Dialogues of the Buddha* in 1919 and 1921. In 1899-1900 he visited the holy Buddhist sites in India. Following his visit he produced a remarkable work *Buddhist India* (1903). This was a pioneer study surveying the social and political conditions in which Buddhism arose.

He passed away in 1922. Among the tributes to him were:

The Anagarika Dharmapala: 'When will England give birth again to a man like Rhys Davids? He gave life to those indifferent to religion. By the publication of Pali texts, in Roman characters, he brought the *Buddhavaccana* within the reach of the poor scholar. His name will never be forgotten by the Pali student'.

Dr W A de Silva: 'His was not mere scholarship, eminent as it was; his was the opportunity, and he took it to expound the word of the Dhamma of the Great Master. And we in Ceylon had in him one who not only loved the Island and the Sinhalese, but one who was able to place before the world the best we have ever acquired in our history'.

Another notable, British Pali scholar was Frank Lee Woodward. He was born in England in 1871. He showed a natural aptitude for the Classics and for modern languages and was also a gifted sportsman. He won a classical scholarship to Sidney Sussex College, Cambridge and passed the Classical Tripos with honours. He taught at several schools and then became Second Master at Stamford school. There he devoted much time to study Eastern and Western philosophy and Pali and Sanskrit. He joined the Theosophical Society in 1902. He described becoming a member of it as 'the most important event of his life', for it led to his acceptance of Buddha's teachings. He wrote to Colonel Olcott offering his services in the East. It was immediately accepted as, at the time, the BTS needed a Headmaster for Mahinda College, Galle.

When he arrived in Galle in 1903, he found the College housed in an old Dutch building in the Fort. The attendance was only 60. Woodward, himself, selected the present site, the land being donated by public-spirited residents. He was not only the architect of the school but also the foreman of works. He was often seen with a trowel in hand among the masons or up the scaffolding. He set a very high standard for the College and it made rapid progress under his direction. He sought no publicity. He was revered for his self-sacrifice, generosity and erudition. One of his many efforts was directed at establishing Sinhalese as a subject for the Cambridge Local examinations. He was a pioneer of the Ceylon University movement.

He used to wear a simple garb of white shirt and white cloth and observe the Eight Precepts on full moon day, setting a noble example to his pupils and neighbours. Occasionally, he would offer alms to Buddhist monks in the school hall, himself, serving the meals with great humility and would wash and wipe the feet of the monks as they came in single-file for the alms-giving. He taught various classes everyday as well as dealing with administrative matters. He knew all the pupils by name and gave them all a Shakespearian nickname.

He translated for the Pali Text Society. In 1936 the Society published 15 volumes of a complete translation of the *Digha*, *Majhima*, *Samyutta* and *Anguttara Nikayas*. He, himself translated six of the volumes and gave help with the seventh. He also translated two Minor Anthologies in the Sacred

Books of the Buddhist series *Udana* and *iti-vuttaka*. He left Sri Lanka in 1919 for Tasmania where he continued editing and translating Pali texts. He published *Some Sayings of the Buddha*, which was a collection of passages from the four great Nikayas and *Pictures of Buddhist Ceylon and Other Papers* which describes Buddhist life in Sri Lanka.

Sir Robert Chalmers was another eminent Pali scholar who was Governor of Ceylon from 1913-1915. He was born in London and went up to Oxford in 1877 with a Classical scholarship but later read Natural Sciences. After leaving Oxford, he entered the Treasury, eventually becoming Permanent Secretary in 1911. Chalmers was attracted to Pali by the enthusiasm of Rhys Davids whose pupil he became. He joined the Pali

Text Society in 1894 and published a paper in the Journal of the Royal Asiatic Society entitled 'the Madhura Sutta – concerning caste'. The next year in the same journal he published another paper on the 'Nativity of the Buddha'. He then took over the task of translating the Jataka Tales from Rhys Davids. The first volume was translated by Chalmers in 1895 containing Jatakas 1 to 150.

Chalmers arrived in Ceylon as Governor in 1913. His fame as a Pali scholar had preceded him and local scholars, particularly Buddhist monks, were delighted. One of his first public engagements was to preside over a prize-giving at Vidyodaya Pirivena. As he had studied Pali in Roman script, the monks thought that he would not be able to enunciate Pali words and arranged for an interpreter to translate his English speech to Sinhalese. But to their utter amazement, he replied to their elaborate Pali address of welcome with an extempore speech in choice Pali, flawlessly enunciating every word. He concluded his half hour address by saying: 'May this noble Pali language ever flourish in Sri Lanka'. Later he decided to bring out an edition of the Ceylonese Commentaries, which he proposed to call the Aluvihara Edition. As he explained in an address at the Vidyodaya Pirivena in February 1915: 'I shall do myself the pleasure of paying the printer's bill for the thousand copies of the two volumes of the Dhammarana Edition of the Papanca Sudani and secondly asking the Ceylon Branch of the Royal Asiatic Society to accept as a gift from me a thousand copies, the sale proceeds of which will form a reproductive fund for the future publication of Pitakas and Atthakathas by Ceylon's most eminent scholars in our Aluvihara Edition. Mark the name 'Aluvihara Edition', to which I attach special value, both as recognising a debt to those Ceylon scholars who laboured at Aluvihara, two thousand years ago, and also as recording our own aspirations in these latter days to follow in their footsteps by giving Ceylon, in printed form, a rescension worthy alike of Ceylon's traditions and her scholarship today'. The Society accepted the offer in November 1915 and the proceeds were kept in a special fund called: 'The Chalmers Oriental Text Fund'. In 1914, Marie Musaeus-Higgins dedicated her book *Jatakalama* to Chalmers. Chalmers wrote a paper for *The Ceylon Antiquary and Literary Register* in July 1915 on Buddhaghosa and his work. Unfortunately, when Chalmers was recalled to England in 1915 after the 1915 riots, which he mishandled, all his constructive plans for Ceylon's pre-eminence for Pali scholarship had to be abandoned, with only one book, the Papanca-sudani of the Majjhima, being published. Fortunately, the work begun under the inspiration of Chalmers was not destined to be left undone, and was progressed with funds left in the will of Simon Hewavitarne.

He was appointed Master of Peterhouse College, Cambridge in 1924. During his Mastership, in 1927, he published the *Further Dialogues of the Buddha* which were translations from the Majjhima Nikaya in two volumes. He then produced his last work of scholarship – a metrical translation of the Sutta Nipata, the earliest teaching of the Buddha in Pali verse. He showed considerable literary skills in his translation, sought out good English equivalents for the technical terms of Buddhism and cut short remorseless repetitions. He was appointed President of the Royal Asiatic Society in 1922. He continued to take an interest in Pali studies in Sri Lanka after he left. He donated his fine Pali library to Miss I B Horner, the then Librarian of Newnham College, Cambridge. He passed away in November 1938.

It is remarkable that someone who was not a Buddhist, did not live in a Buddhist country, nor was employed to do so, would devote nearly forty years of his adult life to translating or editing about two thousand pages of Pali text.

The British fascination for Sri Lanka's sacred literature led to the texts being translated into the vernacular and published in printed books. Far more scholars could now read and make a detailed study of them. For the first time academic papers were published both in Sri Lanka and in the West on Sri Lanka's cultural heritage. Based on these, more general books were written on Buddhism and Sri Lanka's ancient history. Initially, these publications were read by the educated classes but later booklets, magazines and newspaper articles appeared which the whole population could read. The introduction of modern printing meant that instead of having a few copies of these texts in pansalas, publications based on them could be found in every home in the land. The focus of the British on analysing these texts encouraged Sri Lankans to do the same. As G P Malalasekera noted in *The Pali Literature of Ceylon*: 'This brief account of the literary revival in Ceylon during the last century would be incomplete without some reference, at least, to the exertions of the Europeans in the Island, missionaries, civil servants and others, whose researches it was that first brought home to the Ceylonese the glories of their own literature, when many of them had begun to treat it with neglect'. The establishment of the learned societies such as the Ceylon Branch of the Royal Asiatic Society enabled both the British and Sri Lankans to share their enthusiasm for Sri Lanka's cultural heritage. The British involvement also meant that these activities took place in Britain and elsewhere. When Anagarika Dharmapala came to Britain to establish a Buddhist temple, he found a country where the educated classes were well-read on Buddhism, members of learned societies had for decades shared their interest in cultures of Asia and academics in universities had been studying the ancient languages of the East for nearly a century. This was a fertile soil in which the seeds of Buddhism could germinate and flower.

When assessing the overall legacy of the British for Buddhism in Sri Lanka, it is evident that after a few decades of difficulty caused by the insensitivity of the early Colonial Authorities and the activities of the missionaries, Buddhism gained considerably and revived from the middle of the 19$^{th}$ century onwards. The establishment of a central government and peaceful conditions enabled the British to direct the resources of the State to establish the Archaeological Survey of Ceylon which restored ancient Buddhist cities after centuries of decay. The challenges from the missionaries encouraged the Buddhists to focus on their sacred texts, determine the essence of their faith and make resolute efforts to expound the dhamma to the people. The availability of printed books greatly increased the laity's understanding of their religion and culture. There was a flowering of cultural interest with the revival of vernacular learning and Oriental studies. With the study of Sri Lanka's ancient history, its ancient old languages and religion, the Sri Lankans themselves began to look back with pride to their glorious past. For the first time in centuries the people of Lanka could visit the ruined cities and gaze with awe at the grandeur of their bygone heritage. Most of all, they could now go on pilgrimage to all the holy places associated with Buddhism in India.

It is interesting to reflect that the first major expansion of Buddhism took place during the reign of the Emperor Asoka; the second during the period of the British Empire. It is rare in history for people of one faith to do so much to facilitate the expansion of another faith. Buddhists everywhere owe a profound debt of gratitude to these curious Saxons.

# Bibliography


## Primary Sources

Allen C (2002) The Buddha and the Sahibs, John Murray
Bell N B, Bell H M (1993) H C P Bell, Archaeologist of Ceylon and The Maldives, Archetype Publications
Chakrabarti D K (2001) The History of Indian Archaeology from the beginning to 1947, Munshiram Manoharlal Publishers
De Silva K M (2005) A History of Sri Lanka, Vijitha Yapa Publications
Singh U (2006) The Discovery of Ancient India, Permanent Black
Wijesekera N (1990) History of the Department of Archaeology (Volume 1), Archaeological Department, Sri Lanka

## Secondary Sources

Ahir D C (2000) Buddhist Shrines in India, B R Paperbacks
Ali A U (1925) The Making of India, A&C Black Ltd.
Archaeological Survey of India (1953) Ancient India No.9 – Special Jubilee Number, Archaeological Survey of India
Bastiampillai B (1968) The Administration of Sir William Gregory, Tisara Prakasakayo
Bell H C P (1911) Archaeological Survey of Ceylon – North Central, Northern and Central Provinces, Annual Report 1907, Archaeological Survey of Ceylon
Blakiston, J F (1935) Address on Occasion of the Presentation of Buddhist Relics to the Maha Bodhi Society at Sarnath on 10th November 1935, Journal of the Maha Bodhi Society, December, 1935
Cumming J Sir (1939) Revealing India's Past, The India Society
Das S (2014) 200 Years of the Indian Museum 1814–2014, The Indian Museum
De Silva H (2008) Uncovering Sri Lanka's Past: the beginnings in the 19th century, The Triple Gem blog, 22 March 2008
De Silva P H D H (2000) Colombo Museum 100 Years 1877-1977, Department of National Museums, Sri Lanka

De Silva W A (1910-12) A List of Pali Books Printed in Ceylon in Singhalese Characters, Journal of the Pali Text Society, 133-135

— — (1924) The Status and Influence of Buddhism in Ceylon, Conference on Some Living Religions of the Empire

— — A (1931) History of Buddhism in Ceylon, Buddhistic Studies (Edited by B C Law)

— — A (1938) Catalogue of Palm Leaf Manuscripts in the Library of the Colombo Museum, Colombo Museum

— — A (1940) A Cycle of National Progress, Buddhist Theosophical Society Diamond Jubilee Souvenir

Devendra D T (1940) The Buddhist Revival, Buddhist Theosophical Society Diamond Jubilee Souvenir

De Zoysa L (1887) Notes on Certain Jatakas Relative to the Sculptures Recently Discovered in Northern India, Journal of the Ceylon Branch Royal Asiatic Society

Dharmadasa K N O (2004) George Turnour: The man who brought world fame to the Mahavamsa, *Island* newspaper, 4 January 2004

Dharmapala Anagarika (1900) History of The Maha-Bodhi Temple at Bodh Gaya, Mahabodhi Society

— — (1915) Report of the Maha Bodhi Society from 1891 to 1915

— — (1921) The Re-establishment of Buddhism in India, The Buddhist Annual of Ceylon

Hazra K L (2009) The Rise and Decline of Buddhism in India, Munshiram Manoharlal Publishers

Her Majesty's Stationery Office (1870) Correspondence between The Governor of Ceylon and The Secretary of State for Colonies with reference to the preparation of a Descriptive Catalogue of Pali, Sinhalese and Sanskrit Manuscripts to be found in the libraries of the pansalas and other places in Ceylon

Ievers R W (1890) Letter from the Government Agent, Anuradhapura on the Restorations of the Abhayagiri and Mirisawetiya Dagabas, Skeen, Government Printer, Colombo

Jayatilaka D B (1940) Christian Methods of Conversion, Buddhist Theosophical Society Diamond Jubilee Souvenir

Kirthisinghe B P, Amarasuriya M P (1981) Colonel Olcott His service to Buddhism, Buddhist Publications Society

Majumdar B (2007) A Guide to Sarnath, Pilgrim Publications

Majmudar R C, Raychaudhuri H C, Datta K (1965) An Advanced History of India, Macmillan and Company Limited

Malalasekera G P (1973) The Pali Literature of Ceylon, Buddhist Publications Society

Marshall J Sir(1924) The Monuments of Sanchi, The Great India Peninsula Railway

Mendis G C (2005) Ceylon Under the British, Asian Educational Services

Ministry of Information and Broadcasting Government of India (1967) Archaeology in India

Pakeman S A (1948) A Hundred Years of the Royal Asiatic Society, Journal of the Ceylon Branch of the Royal Asiatic Society, 1-12

Parker P L (1898) The Most Remarkable Fortress in the World, Harmsworth Magazine, Vol1, 274-9

Peiris W (1973) The Western Contribution to Buddhism, Motilal Banarsidass

Piyadasa T G (1985) Libraries in Sri Lanka - Origin and History, Sri Satguru Publications

Pratt J B (1928) The Pilgrimage of Buddhism, The Macmillan Company

Rasheed A (1907) The Traveller's Companion, The Railways Board

Roy S (1996) The Story of Indian Archaeology 1784 – 1947, Archaeological Survey of India

Sahni D R (1917) Guide to Buddhist Ruins of Sarnath, Archaeological Survey of India

Salgado U (2004) In Search of Suttas and a Buried Religion, Vesak Lipi

Sangharakshita B (1983) Anagarika Dharmapala - A Biographical Sketch, Buddhist Publications Society

The Asiatic Society (2014) Two Hundred and Twenty-Five Years of the Asiatic Society, The Asiatic Society

Trevithick A (2006) The Revival of Buddhist Pilgrimage at Bodh Gaya (1811-1949), Motilal Banarsidass Publications

Wickremeratne A (1984) The Genesis of an Orientalist: Thomas Rhys Davids in Sri Lanka, Motilal Banarsidass

Williams H (1953) Ceylon Pearl of the East, Robert Hale Ltd

Wright A (1907) Twentieth Century Impressions of Ceylon, Lloyd's Greater Britain Publishing Company Ltd.

# Index